TOMAS

James Palumbo

QUARTET

First published in 2009 by
Quartet Books Limited
A member of the Namara Group
27 Goodge Street, London W1T 2LD

A catalogue record for this book
is available from the British Library

ISBN   978 0 7043 7158 3

Typeset by Antony Gray
Printed and bound in Great Britain by
T J International Ltd, Padstow, Cornwall

WARNING

Reader, beware this book. It's short and small. It fits into your pocket and you can read it at leisure in any public place or alone at night. It looks like so many other books. You may think that, if the author's any good, the story will help you escape the world around you; you can drift into another place, better or worse, according to your mood. This is precisely the danger. Do not trust appearances: below these black printed words, spread page over page, lies a vision of the world that will alarm the majority, revolt the sensitive and obliterate the prudish.

This book will work on your brain like a vaccine: you'll read a few lines and, I suspect, rebel instantly against its contents. You'll be shocked, disgusted, horrified that such ideas are allowed in print. I can already hear many detractors referring to bad taste or sheer madness: for me these are compliments. I trust, however, that I'll have the last word. Some among you will survive its reading and, as a result, may acquire a new perspective on our world. Excess of imagination, passion, outrage, death, love, greed and vice often provides a clearer view of life.

TOMAS

You have been warned. This isn't a light-hearted romance, nor a work of science fiction. It's simply a tale that shouldn't be read too seriously. It makes fun of our society in a way that will delight teenagers while disturbing everyone else. But I'm confident that my message, protected by the crudity of its tone, remains unimpaired: it recounts without pity the bonfire of vanities that has become our daily grind.

You'll meet Tomas. As you will see, he starts life rather poorly; a bit of a violent man, who wishes to eradicate all that he disapproves of. He goes on to battle many of the issues so troubling to our modern world – sex, love, money, success, failure. Ultimately he confronts life's greatest enigma; how to be more than a great nothing?

So – who knows? – should you traverse the murky waters of shock, horror and disgust, you might get to like Tomas. Stranger still, he may even help you.

THE FRENCH RIVIERA

page 9

PARIS

page 69

CANNES

page 135

THE FRENCH RIVIERA

ILLUSTRATION ON
THIS PAGE

1

ILLUSTRATION ON
THIS PAGE

A champagne-fuelled jungle is in for a surprise . . .

Tomas walks into a club in an exclusive resort at the height of the season. All the boys are wearing white shirts, the uniform of party boys, with oversized collars. These are so big they flop down to their waists like some sea creature's fleshy protrusion. They also sport gigantic watches, weighing down their wrists like anchors. All of them wear sunglasses even though they're indoors and it's night.

The girls hobble on skyscraper stilettos like newborn giraffes unsure of their footing. All have breasts so enormous that they have to be supported on mobile trolleys on which they push their appendages about in front of them. Every few minutes, the girls throw back their heads and laugh in unison. They're alive with pleasure.

The air is thick with smoke and vibrates to the tinny noise of the club sound system. At half-hour intervals the music stops and an uplifting theme from a science-fiction film fills the room. The crowd roars as a giant champagne bottle, a sparkler fizzing from its decapitated neck, is carried through the club. The baying delight at this spectacle belies a reverential awe; who could be so magnificent as to order this €20,000 leviathan? That's it, follow the bottle: let's see which table it's destined for.

TOMAS

The champagne reaches journey's end. A pack of hyenas in the uniform of white shirts with oversized collars laugh and shout as if to say, 'Look at us! Look at us!' or, more particularly, 'Look at me! Look at me!' They, too, are alive with pleasure.

Everything now seems in slow motion to Tomas: the music is stifled, like a disc slowing down on a gramophone; the hyenas bay but you can only hear them at half speed; the breast trolleys manoeuvre slowly: blink and they've moved – or maybe they haven't?

Tomas steps into the slow-motion scene, ties his hair into a knot and pulls two guns from under his jacket. One is a crude Chicago-in-the-gangster-days tommy gun making a rat-a-tat-tat noise. The other is a slick modern weapon with a silencer, so all you can hear is the thud of bullets. Moving from left to right, Tomas sprays the room with a look of calm concentration, like a child taking an exam. Everything's still at half speed, except now the music has stopped altogether and the only sounds are thuds, glass breaking, people falling.

The scene returns to normal, the slow-motion button turned off. The guns have done their work. There's a curious haze in the room. Glass splinters as survivors try to move, there are moans and sudden bangs as people and objects fall over.

Although the police and medics arrive fast, the resort isn't set up to deal with an apocalypse and Tomas slips away in no particular hurry.

THE FRENCH RIVIERA

How to seek approval . . .

The next day, Tomas takes himself to an expensive beach club, where he looks out of place in his ragged T-shirt and shorts and Bible-prophet sandals. The manager arches a disapproving eyebrow as he pays the €100 entry fee and goes to find a white sun lounger.

'Can I have one that's more pretentious?' Tomas asks an attendant.

'Of course, Sir, but only on condition that you make yourself ridiculous.'

'That's no problem,' replies Tomas.

Tomas is conducted to a sunbed ten times the size of the rest. There's no point to this colossus, which is far less comfortable than a normal lounger on to which you can fit snugly. Tomas slides to the middle, unsheltered from the sun by the umbrella. He strips off his clothes and wraps his lower body in a large white towel. He is already brown from spending so much time outdoors but soon his sinewy chest begins to sizzle in the heat.

'Can I have a giant umbrella?' asks Tomas.

'No,' the attendant replies, 'that would put things into proportion and make you look normal.'

Tomas decides to perch on the side. 'Is this good enough?' he asks.

'I'm sorry, Sir,' the attendant says. 'You look pathetic and the deal was ridiculous.'

'OK,' says Tomas. 'Bring me an oversized champagne bottle but make sure I can carry it.'

'Immediately, Sir,' says the attendant.

ILLUSTRATION ON
THIS PAGE

2

ILLUSTRATION ON
THIS PAGE

Minutes later he returns, carrying a monster bottle. A second attendant brings a glass. 'I don't need that,' says Tomas and waves the glass away.

The bottle is uncorked with a pop and handed to Tomas. The attendants stand to one side as Tomas takes it in his arms.

He ambles over to the pool, watched by the inhabitants of the sun loungers, and kicks off his sandals. 'Go on,' shouts Tomas to the attendants. 'Turn up the music. Turn it up real good.'

The attendants comply: the background Balearic beats rise to a deafening roar. The music also increases in tempo. Tomas didn't ask for this but now a wave of ridiculousness is gathering its own momentum. Everyone props themselves up to watch.

Because of the speed of the music Tomas can't segue into the rhythm. He has to jump in and start dancing like a maniacal fool. He shakes the champagne bottle and sprays his audience with a plume of sticky froth. 'Ha! Ha! Ha!' he squeals. 'Ha! Ha! Ha!' they reply.

'How'm I doing?' Tomas asks the attendants.

'Oh, very well, Sir, you look ridiculous.'

Through all the noise and excitement, Tomas hears an invisible voice in his head. 'If you're to experience the full horror of the situation, Tomas,' it says, 'you must sacrifice yourself to it Messiah-like.'

The next step up from ridiculous is ludicrous.

Tomas begins a barnyard dance, like an Iowa farmer at the harvest-day ball. This should be performed to music at half the speed of the balearic beats, so his efforts appear all the more absurd. The dance consists of stomping one leg up at a right angle while moving both arms up and down in parallel, with elbows pointing out. The weight is then transferred to the other foot and the process repeated. This is accompanied by a synchronised bobbing of the head in and out, up and down, like a rooster calling the dawn chorus. These jerky movements loosen Tomas's towel, which falls to the ground, so he carries on his performance naked, his penis flailing. Because the dance is impossible to perform holding an overweight champagne bottle, Tomas drops it; but the bottle is animated by the situation, refuses to smash and floats in the air, a silent spectator of events.

'Look at me,' whoops Tomas, 'I'm having such fun. I'm spraying champagne. I'm dancing. I'm cool, swaying my hips and exposing myself. I'm alive with pleasure.'

'Ha! Ha! Ha!' roar the crowd approvingly. They, too, are alive with pleasure.

After his performance, Tomas rests on his tennis-court-sized sun lounger. For some reason it's grown during his performance. He suspects it has something to do with his rooster imitation. He has pushed ridiculous to the territorial hinterland of ludicrous and the lounger rewards him by swelling to a still more incredible size.

TOMAS

The dangers of melting butter . . .

The beach-club restaurant is an extravagant array of polished wood tables under white parasols, adorned by the deep purples and subtle pinks of Mediterranean summer flowers. The menu offers grilled fish, huge baskets of crudités, fruits, pasta and wines of every sort.

Because it's hot, the boys aren't wearing their full white-shirt uniform; only the collar attached to the neck, which flops down to form two useless wings. You've heard of shirts with no collars. Well, these are collars with no shirts. While there's no sartorial point to them, they define the central characteristic of their owners – uselessness.

The girls are busy trolleying their fake breasts as they move between the tables; trolleys and breasts are accentuated in the daylight. The nightclub trolleys were black, in a way discreet despite their size and function. The beach trolleys are more conspicuous, adorned by large white towels on which morning-tanned breasts flop in gentle repose.

Tomas finds a table and asks for a menu. He's now re-clothed in his shorts and a fifty-euro souvenir T-shirt featuring the club's logo, a bucket of sick, which was given to him as a reward for his poolside dance. A trolley-pushing blonde parks at the table beside him to await her collar-wearing beau.

Tomas is about to summon the waiter when the blonde interposes: 'Waiter! Waiter!'

One immediately appears. 'Madame?' he says.

'My butter's melting. I insist you do something about it.'

'Immediately, madame.'

Tomas thinks carefully about this exchange. His brow creases in concentration and he ties his hair back with a band to think. Before even giving her command the blonde has appropriated the butter. The butter is not described with an impersonal 'the' but a possessive 'my'. By virtue of parking her breasts at the table, the butter has become 'hers'. It may also be that in her language – a special variant of English – every sentence begins with the words 'I', 'me' or 'my'.

The use of the present tense 'is melting' appears to Tomas to be a lesser offence than the past-tense disaster 'has melted'. Had the butter committed this capital crime, Tomas imagines the blonde pressing one of her nipples to activate a siren. Immediately a wail fills the restaurant and defensive barriers rise from the sand. The sky fills with helicopter gunships and American voices announce through loud hailers: 'Attention! The butter has melted. The situation is under control. Do nothing. Stay calm.'

But this catastrophe is averted. The butter is merely melting.

The 'do something about it' is a less alarming proposition but opens up more possibilities. The unimaginative response would be to fetch fresh butter. In doing this the waiter would abdicate his responsibility to save the life of the expiring condiment. A compromise could be to move the parasol to shield the butter from the sun's melting beams. But this might incur the blonde's wrath. Etiquette demands new butter. She will accept nothing less. And those breasts weren't constructed to be upset.

Tomas speculates that they have nuclear potential. The French Riviera atomised because a waiter fails to bring fresh butter.

Still Tomas isn't satisfied. One solution is unimaginative, the other defensive. He is urged on by the same invisible voice. 'Are there no scientific or even futuristic possibilities?' it asks.

Tomas chides himself for thinking so one-dimensionally. Sometimes the best solution is the least obvious. Bringing fresh butter or moving the parasol is a child's answer. What about moving the sun or blotting it out altogether?

Of course he realises that this isn't possible. But in the cause of serving the rich and famous, who are always complaining, every expedient must be considered. It may be that the waiter can't provide this solution at present. But in a world of eternal return, where events repeat themselves in perpetuity, all he need do is find a way to live for ever, construct a sun-blotting or -moving technology and wait for the incident to recur. An alternative, of course, is time travel. From some future time or life the waiter can voyage back to this moment with the necessary technical apparatus and deal with the situation. Thus . . .

'My butter's melting. I insist you do something about it.'

'Immediately, madame.'

The waiter produces a pistol from his pocket and fires an almost silent shot between the parasols into the air. Instantly the sea begins to froth and foam. There's a groaning sound like the girders of a bridge breaking free and a spacecraft with massive distended arms rises from the ocean. Within seconds it has jumped into hyperspace and is barrelling towards the sun.

'Moved or blotted out, madame?' the waiter enquires.

'Moved will do.'

The waiter fires another shot. The arms of the space-craft stretch outward and lock into position at both extremities of the sun. A button is pressed ten thousand miles above earth and they clamp on. Seconds later, the sun has been moved.

'May I recommend the fish?' the waiter asks.

'I need time to think,' the blonde replies, waving him away. 'This butter incident has upset me.'

'Of course, madame,' the waiter responds. 'Would it help if I blew my brains out? The butter almost melting was a disaster. It might make you feel better were I to kill myself.'

The blonde fails to answer. She's exhausted by the drama. The pop of the pistol shots disturbed her imperceptibly, but disturbed her nevertheless. She looks at the butter, which is melting no longer, and remembers that she doesn't even like butter; why on earth has she gone to all this trouble?

Tomas balances in his mind these solutions to the blonde's problem. A final possibility occurs to him. He takes out his weapons and sprays the restaurant. He finishes with the blonde, who slumps forward into the butter and ruins it anyway.

TOMAS

A higher calling . . .

Tomas wanders down to the port to seek solace in its azure waters. He's disappointed that his killing spree has had so little effect. Although word has spread, people continue as normal, unperturbed by the lone gunman who is providing important morality lessons via his annihilating weapons.

Tomas has been sent mad by Shit TV. Shit TV is the biggest media network in world history, with an audience of billions. After years of tedious reality shows – singing competitions, jungle-survival programmes, business-apprentice shoot-outs – people want more. Shit TV is the answer.

Shit TV broadcasts globally twenty-four hours per day. Dozens of shows cover everything that is most base and nasty in the world – trafficking, violence, perversions of every sort; in short, shit: a celebration of the fetid trough of dirty Russian money, footballers abusing adolescent girls and bankers raping the planet. And why not? If the ship's sinking, let the people watch.

Programmes include 'Fuck Me for A Lie', in which pretend film producers trick girls into sex; 'Fat Ballet: Eat My Fat', featuring obese dancers who perform before an audience in hysterics and then do something too disgusting to describe; and the ever popular original, 'Shit TV Show', of which Tomas is the star.

Shit TV has also achieved a technological breakthrough. Millions of TV sets are fitted with a connecting tube and buttons marked 'smell' and 'shit'. Viewers watching 'I'm a Raw-Sewage Swimmer' can heighten their olfactory pleasure by pressing 'smell'. A surprising number use the 'shit' button.

Tomas enjoys cult status worldwide. He's an object of desire to millions of girls who are obsessed with his Messiah-like looks. Still more boys want to copy his devil-be-damned attitude and hippy-chic style. His job, like his appearance, is simplicity itself. He pitches up with a camera crew at major events – royal weddings, political swearing-ins, football finals. Within full view of the ceremony, event or podium in question he drops his trousers and defecates, to the unbridled joy of a global audience. He then speeds off, trousers and other unpleasantries trailing.

St Paul was converted on the road to Damascus; Tomas in the Emperor Napoleon's tomb in the centre of Paris on a cloudless summer's day, at a ceremony to mark the great man's birthday. Having reconnoitered the chamber meticulously, Tomas leapt forward at the critical moment to perform his act when he was dazzled by a sunbeam streaming into the tomb from a dome window. It was a moment of incandescent light, beauty and joy. An invisible voice inside Tomas's head told him he'd been called to a higher purpose. The world was tipping into a foul sewer of despond. Drastic, even murderous action was needed to awaken society before it was too late. It would be righteous to take it: although he had erred, even the lowliest may rise, and the sinner become a saint. This was his task: a sacred quest to save the world.

Numbed but certain of his mission, Tomas arrived on the French Riviera a few hours later.

✧

TOMAS

The old enemy awakes . . .

The Russian Great Bear stirs in his wintry lair. Although it's summer on the French Riviera, he prefers his cave of perpetual cold. He has spent years here healing his wounds, some as deep as the revenge he's planning.

The beast's fur is mottled, criss-crossed with scars of war and defeat. His shoulders are stooped and he walks across his lair on stocky legs with an awkward gait; a slow shaggy giant. This only serves to deceive: his strength has returned and he's fast if he needs to be.

Russia's loss of the Cold War two decades ago dealt a shattering blow to the Great Bear and sent him into his hibernation of depression and disgrace. There he slept, his pain anaesthetised by the cold. Finally, he woke and began to plot his vengeance from his kingdom of ice and snow.

He recalls the early days of his plan, the seeming impossibility of joining battle with the West once again. Force was useless; in running the arms race Russia had buckled and collapsed. He had to find a more subtle means. But what? Communism was in chaos, everything he believed in swept away by the West's devastating economic tsunami.

Then it occurred to him. What was the opposite of communism and played the West at its own game? A menace difficult to anticipate and impossible to resist. The answer was so simple that it could be described in a single word. A commodity which after only a few years was already debauching Western values and behaviour.

Money. Russian money and all it brings: envy, the corruption of scruples, social dysfunction. Western bankers accept a Russian rouble without questioning its origin. Oligarchs, the new weapons of war, are welcomed with open arms by society, irrespective of their backgrounds. Yachts, mansions and jetted-in prostitutes are envied as symbols of the Great Bear's new empire. Previously good people now bow in submission to the vulgarities of Russian taste, behaviour and power.

The beast's black eyes fix on the boulder that serves as a door to his cave. The rot is set, he thinks, as sure as stone. Soon it will be time for his final plan.

He pads over to the boulder and turns his mind from his great design to a seemingly microscopic issue: reports of a gunman on a killing spree on the French Riviera, the world headquarters of decadent and licentious behaviour, where Russian yachts patrol offshore like battleships and oligarchs command armies of hitmen and hookers. No wonder the gunman, styling himself as a celestial avenger, has chosen this latter-day Sodom and Gomorrah.

Normally, such news would be inconsequential to the Great Bear. A lone killer, clearly mad, touting automatic weapons and a moral message with no hope of success. A few dozen deaths of society types, including some Russians. So what?

But the beast's long hibernation hasn't dulled his instincts, if anything the opposite. His senses are as sharp as the cold. For the first time in two decades, he takes a fateful decision. He rolls back the boulder and steps out of his cave. His retinue, camped outside, is shocked. The Great Bear never leaves his lair; his enemies must come to him.

TOMAS

His attendants scatter in fear and confusion. Ignoring the commotion, the Great Bear raises himself high on his hind legs like a predator hoping to catch the scent of blood in the wind. He tilts his head back sharply and with a vertical snout sniffs the snow-and-rain-drenched air with short, sharp breaths which billow puffs of steam above his head. He's right. Something's wrong.

Pride comes before a fall . . .

A helicopter clatters overhead on its descent to the port's landing pad. Tomas watches as its owner tumbles out. He has a normal trunk but an enormous stomach, which Tomas imagines is detachable. His belly is so big that its top is parallel to his mouth and he has to shout to be heard. Perhaps he has had a treatment at a Swiss clinic to distribute weight only to his stomach. This allows him to eat as much as he wants while leaving him lithe elsewhere. His stomach, being detachable, provides the ultimate in corporal flexibility. Maybe he leaves it on a cot by his bed at night and only brings it out during the day for meals and for show.

The detachable-stomach man pauses on the step of his helicopter. He's surrounded by journalists and photographers. 'Boss Olgarv,' shouts a reporter, 'are you frightened of the killer?' Russia's oligarch-in-chief, arriving to investigate the situation and do a little business, doesn't reply. Instead he snaps, 'Wait!' to the photographers. He flips a mobile to his ear. 'OK,' he obliges. The photographers get to work. His imaginary telephone conversation adds to his magnificence. This is the picture he wants, exiting his helicopter, eyes narrowed on the horizon – a man of vision as well as wealth; the world transfixed by what he might be saying: 'Buy it now, damn it!' 'OK, sue the bastards.' 'Yes. One hundred million euros, not a euro more.'

The fat Russian walks towards a yacht, mobile still clamped to his ear, photographers calling his name, a small crowd gathered to watch and admire. Tomas is prepared to provide another morality lesson but holds back for a moment out of curiosity. At the raised gangplank of his boat, Boss Olgarv reaches into his pocket. This is it, the climax of the show. He withdraws his hand with a flourish and brandishes a clicker, which he points at the boat. The crowd and press pack fall silent. 'Click. Click.' Nothing happens. He shakes it and aims in a different direction. 'Click. Click.' And again, 'Click. Click.' The gangplank, whose purpose in life is to descend, permitting its owner a magnificent exit, remains stubbornly erect.

A bead of sweat forms on Boss Olgarv's brow. Someone in the crowd sniggers. The commander of men and worlds can't command a plank. The finale isn't going to plan.

As he waits on the dockside, face reddening, an aide calls from the balustrade of the yacht. 'Boss. We need you on board as soon as possible. The video conference is about to start. The American bankers are waiting.'

'Idiot,' he replies, the walls of his cool beginning to crumble. 'This fucking thing won't work. Get me on board.'

TOMAS

The aide blanches and disappears, reappearing with an engineer in blue overalls, who attempts to entice the gangplank to obey by way of a manual lever. Disembodied grunts, huffs and puffs and a 'Fuck!' float over the yacht rail. The gangplank maintains its phallic posture, as if it has sighted a female gangplank across the harbour and is sending a friendly message.

'Boss. We must get you on board for the call. We could lose the deal. We'll use the hoist.'

Boss Olgarv assesses his options. Humiliation, slung on board like a pack animal, or losing a deal? A nanosecond later he beckons for the hoist to be lowered. A mechanical arm emerges from the yacht bow, a harness dangling from it.

'Put your arms through the straps,' calls the aide. 'Secure the belt around your waist, click the safety buckle and we'll do the rest.'

Boss Olgarv complies. A thousand trumpets sound the collapse of his citadel of self-esteem.

Tomas is mesmerised by the spectacle of this harnessed animal aloft. Even a cow would have more dignity; surrender to its fate, perhaps emitting a moo of complaint. Tomas wants the fat Russian to moo. But God is in his heaven – something better happens.

Halfway to the deck, still dangling in mid-air, the hoist stutters and stops. It's an industrial machine tested to destruction by Teutonic robots. Perhaps today it senses an ego heavier than any physical burden and gives up. The fat Russian panics.

Twisting, turning. 'No, Boss. No.' Flailing, failing.

'Boss. Stop. No.' The safety buckle surrenders its captive and the azure waters welcome an unfamiliar creature into their enveloping depths.

Brilliant bankers at their best . . .

The crowd rushes to the water's edge.

Cameras train on a bobbing head and there is a tropical rainstorm of clicks. But what's this spherical object floating nearby?

'It's his stomach,' a cry goes up. 'He's got a detachable stomach. Look, it's so fat it's floating.'

Even though he's half submerged, Tomas sees the look of horror on Boss Olgarv's face. If only the depths would swallow him up. But this is all too much fun, so the depths decide not to.

Boss Olgarv makes another rapid calculation. Under maritime law, a salvaging party can lay claim to a stricken vessel, jettisoned cargo containers and any random object floating on the surface of the water.

'Save my stomach!' he shrieks. 'Leave me. Hoist it up. Do it.'

What presence of mind to save his stomach, thinks Tomas.

Since the stomach is now unencumbered by its owner's ego, the hoist decides to cooperate and the stomach flops with a dramatic flourish on to the deck, the survivor of an ocean disaster. The next problem is how to board without his stomach in full view of the world's press. There's only one possibility other than time travel. He must swim round to the seaward side of the yacht, which, owing to its vastness, will take precious minutes.

'Boss, the call must start now,' shouts his aide in desperation.

'Improvise, fuck you,' comes the reply as he sets off on his journey, unsupported by the dirigible ballast of his belly.

Moments later, the aide is in a video-conference room addressing a screen of smart-looking American bankers.

'Gentlemen, good afternoon,' he begins. 'We're having some technical problems at this end. The camera's been knocked by the pitch of the boat and you'll only be able to see part of the Boss.'

'No problem,' the chief banker replies.

'Also,' continues the aide, 'we'll lose sound in a few moments, so he'll signal his wishes to you by way of bodily movement.'

'OK, no problem.'

The aide steps to one side and the bankers recognise Boss Olgarv's stomach propped up in a chair at the conference table. It fills the screen impressively.

'Boss Olgarv, good afternoon to you,' says the chief banker. 'We've been studying the acquisition opportunity and feel it makes a lot of sense; it's a good fit. We advise you to go ahead; our fee will be two per cent of the deal.'

The aide breaths a sigh of relief. A few years ago, the Boss acquired for nothing a big-scale retailer in Russia catering for teenage girls. Now it's magically worth billions. The bankers have recommended that he buys a complementary business. He sneaks behind the stomach and wobbles it to signal assent.

'That's great news, Boss,' says the chief banker. 'We'll start the paperwork. Just a moment, please, we need to go offline for a minute.'

Again the stomach wobbles.

The chief banker pushes the mute on his conference phone and turns to his team. 'Boys, there's something going on here. Back me up.'

'Sorry about that, Boss,' he continues. 'We'd like your take on another good fit. It's . . . er . . . a slaughter business, countrywide, with dozens of processing units. We've been thinking – say a teenage girl buys a pink skirt, matching jacket and some pretty accessories, she gets a coupon at the sales counter for one of the slaughterhouses. She goes to the nearest one, hands in her coupon and gets a big chunk of bloody meat or – we don't want to overdo it on the giveaways – maybe some intestines or stinking offal. She takes the bonus gift home along with her pretty pink outfit and everyone's a winner. The slaughter business is a steal and we'll only charge you a ten-per-cent fee. What do you think?'

Panic rises in the aide's chest. He shakes the stomach from behind. But is this a 'yes' shake or a 'no' shake? Isn't it reasonable for the bankers to assume that any shake is a 'yes' shake, since the stomach has already given the first deal its vibrating assent?

'Fantastic, Boss,' says the senior banker. 'We'll take that as a yes – legally recorded on video, of course – and get on with the paperwork. If you don't mind, Hank has another pitch for you.'

The aide attempts another shake as if to convey a 'no'

but the banking pack is in its stride, closing fast on its disembodied prey.

'This one's a bit left of centre, Boss,' starts Hank, 'but hear me out . . . What we do is go along to some waste-processing plants and buy a whole lot of raw sewage – just as much as we can get our hands on. Then we send off to plants in other countries for their shit. After that, we do some deals in underdeveloped countries that pipe sewage into the sea or rivers to get hold of their shit and we buy as much of it as possible. Finally we at the bank save all our own shit just for you. So here's the deal. After twelve months or so you've got this massive pile of shit, probably the biggest pile of shit ever in the history of the world. And our fee will be fifty per cent of all the money we spend to buy the shit, so that's a great deal for you. What do you think?'

The aide knows he must do something to halt this madness and the destruction of his boss's fortune. Summoning all his strength he gives the stomach a gigantic heave; it wobbles and falls off the chair.

A cheer goes up from the bankers.

'That's great news, Boss,' says the chief banker. 'We never thought we'd knock you off your chair. Let's get the money transferred straight away. Have a great day!'

That night, uninformed of events, Boss Olgarv goes to bed. He detaches his stomach and pats it goodnight on its sleeping cot. It's not been a good day but – hey – was it so bad? A few embarrassing photos and a dip in the sea?

In his dreams he's back in the ocean, swimming to the seaward side of his yacht. The sky darkens and the sea turns to shit and blood, infested by the innards of dead animals. On the horizon his aide paddles furiously, deaf to his plaintive cries.

Producers, a party and a peanut . . .

Tomas is cheered by the fat Russian's watery baptism and feels like a party. This is easy: the film festival is on and the city is infested with international glitterati who have the same idea.

Getting invited to a party requires mastering three magic words: 'I'm a producer.' Tomas practises in front of the mirror.

'I'm a peanut,' he says to himself out loud.

'No, that's not quite right,' the invisible voice tells him. 'Try again.'

'You're a peanut,' he affirms with confidence.

'Come on, Tomas. That's even worse. Let's get back on track.'

'I could be a producer,' he tries.

'Present tense, Tomas, present tense, not future conditional.'

'I'm a producer.'

Bingo! In no time at all, Tomas has learnt the magic art. He rushes from his room to try it on a stranger in the hotel bar.

'I'm a producer,' he says flawlessly.

'Great,' replies the stranger. 'There's a party tonight. Here's the address. See you there.'

Tomas arrives at the party vibrating with joy at his

new profession. He performs the three-word magic trick on the first few people he meets and only one is addressed as a peanut. This is an impressive result. Word spreads quickly. Tomas is a producer.

In this new capacity, Tomas finds a number of people – for some reason all girls – who wish to be produced. He joins a table of three potentials who, in thoughtful anticipation of a sudden audition, which might involve a costume change, wear an absolute minimum of clothing. There are also three boys at the table. They're producers too. Two are muscular-looking, tanned with white teeth, and appear to be producers of epic romance films; the third is scrawny, with a long face and scruffy clothing – perhaps he produces scarecrow movies?

The dynamic, therefore, is that all three girls wish to be produced – but by only two of the boys. And since a producer is only capable of practising his magic art on one producee at any one time, there's a problem. The girl who fails to win the favour of the two epic-romance producers will end up in a scarecrow movie.

The conversation ranges over the producers' production credits – none – and the producees' acting experience – also none. But the evening is pregnant with promise. The girls lock legs, arms, eyes and expressions with the epic-romance boys.

'Oh yes, that movie's in the bag,' says one.

'There's no question, I've got that script,' says the other.

As the producers are on the verge of deciding which of the producees to produce the scarecrow interjects, 'I don't like the food here.'

A cold drizzle descends on the table. How could this be of any interest to his fellow artists? Silly old scarecrow. Go off and scare some crows.

'No, I don't like it at all,' he continues, unaffected by the indifference of his professional colleagues. 'It's much better on my boat. My cook's excellent.'

In unison, the three producees turn to face him like soldiers on parade. They stand to attention.

'If one of you girls would be interested in joining me? Or perhaps all of you?'

There's a bang, a puff of smoke, and the two epic-romance producers cease to exist. In a heartbeat, to feature in a scarecrow movie becomes a grail of indescribable holiness to the three producees. Before, they were blind. Hallelujah! Now they can see.

Tomas raises a cynical eyebrow. He suspects it may be time for a further morality lesson. But perhaps his recent annihilation sprees were a little pre-emptory. Besides, he's enjoying watching the ebb and flow of the dance floor. He decides to ask the invisible voice for a translation of the scarecrow's conversation before taking a decision. Thus:

SCARECROW: I don't like the food here.

TRANSLATION: I'm making an anodyne warm-up comment before getting on to what I really want to say.

SCARECROW: No, I don't like it all.

TRANSLATION: I'm creating further anodyne tension to lend greater weight to what's about to come.

SCARECROW:	It's much better on my boat.
TRANSLATION:	I'm rich.
SCARECROW:	My cook's excellent.
TRANSLATION:	I'm very rich.
SCARECROW:	If one of you girls would be interested in joining me?
TRANSLATION:	I want to fuck you.
SCARECROW:	Or perhaps all of you?
TRANSLATION:	I want to fuck you all.

Tomas suspected as much. His biceps bulge as he reaches for his heavy weapons. Just as he loads, he catches a glimpse of something golden across the dance floor. He pockets his guns. As the dance floor pulses to and fro, he catches another glimpse and, a few seconds later, another. Something draws him towards this ethereal glow and he stands up to investigate.

Everything is again in slow motion. The dancers perform their tribal moves at quarter speed; the disco lights are feeble, the music a muddy drone. As Tomas advances, a magic corridor opens up between the dancers and he catches frequent glimpses of the shining thing. Now he has an almost clear view. At last he reaches the end of the corridor. And there she is.

Tomas can't breathe. When his breath returns it's painful. His body is infused with an electric shock that sends tingles to his extremities. His heart literally aches.

She is beautiful beyond words; brown-blonde hair falling unstyled over a wide face, oval brown eyes and a full mouth. She wears a cropped vest over a short tight skirt. She has no bra and he can see the outline of perfect pert breasts.

The glow he noticed across the room is a Mediterranean tan. Although light, it has a magical effect and she radiates like gold. Her legs are smooth and oiled, and she stands with her feet apart, pointing outwards. Her arms hang loose with fingers interlocked before her like a schoolgirl waiting. Her head is lowered but her eyes fix on Tomas.

The slow-motion button is turned off and the club resumes its normal tempo. But in their soporific state, the partygoers have sensed the drama: all eyes are now on Tomas. The music stops and the disco lights swivel to illuminate him standing before his golden angel.

He's in love and everyone knows it.

A microphone appears inches from Tomas's gaping mouth. The first words of his love are to be witnessed by the club, in fact, the whole city. Unbeknownst to the partygoers, speakers sprout mushroom-like across street corners to relay his opening profession of faith in real time.

He shifts from one foot to the other. The club is graveyard still. The whole of the French Riviera holds its breath.

'You're a peanut,' Tomas says.

Truth hurts . . .

'Falling in love wasn't part of the plan,' the invisible voice tells Tomas. But what can he do? The whole point of plans is that they work. Or is it that they don't?

TOMAS

Despite his inauspicious start, Tereza meets Tomas the next day. The street cafe with views over the busy seafront is a perfect setting. They can sit and talk and watch the world go by.

The cafe is busy on this bright Mediterranean afternoon. The waiters stand in a group by the serving area.

'May we please order?' Tomas raises a hand. The waiters look the other way. 'Service?' he mutters feebly.

After several attempts, a waiter comes over and fixes his gaze above Tomas's head, as if he were wearing a silly hat. The waiter doesn't speak but his bored eyes say a bad-tempered 'Yes?'

'Thank you,' says Tomas. 'If we could please . . . '

The waiter's eyes cut him off. To communicate orally would be to show interest, effort, respect. The waiter puts an arm on his hip, slouches a shoulder and says through his eyes, 'Look, there are rules if you want to be here.'

Tomas nods.

'You can either not be served at all,' the speaking eyes continue, 'or I serve you and I'm rude. Alternatively I serve you and you wait a long time. With options two or three – the service options – I bang the plates down loudly.'

Tereza shifts in her chair. 'Is there an option where you're a bit rude and the waiting time is cut in half?' she asks.

'Are you mad?' the eyes flash back. 'Everyone would choose that. You'll be asking me to bang the plates down nicely next. What on earth do you think this place is? By the way, a Coke costs twenty euros, including ice that has no cooling effect and a slice of lemon that tastes of soap.'

Tomas and Tereza choose the rude option – with plates banging – and settle down to talk.

Tereza is even more beautiful in the daylight. She wears a tight-fitting white beach dress and beaded sandals. Her hair is tied up at the back, a few strands falling round her face, and she sports oversized sunglasses.

'Where do we start?' she asks Tomas.

'Let's try an experiment,' he replies. 'When people meet they lie, in order to have sex as quickly as possible. The experiment is not to lie. It's more interesting and original, don't you think?'

'So truth is important?' she asks.

'Yes,' he replies. 'But not in a prudish way. Truth because everyone else lies, so let's not.'

Tereza takes off her sunglasses to look at him unfiltered and reveals a bruise beneath her beautiful eye. She puts the left arm of the glasses into her mouth to think.

'For example,' says Tomas, 'where did you get that bruise? Most girls would make up a story. Will you?'

'I don't know you,' Tereza replies.

'Then my experiment isn't going to work. Which is a relief in a way – I can now start lying to have sex with you.' He leans forward and fixes Tereza with a stare. Now his eyes are speaking – it must be contagious. 'Give it a try, Tereza,' they say.

She takes a moment to examine him. From the club she remembers his height – well over six foot – and the way he moves: an easy glide, strong arms held loose, effortlessly relaxed. Close up, his unkempt appearance contradicts his sharp speech and quick questions. It's clear that the stubble on his high-boned cheeks isn't for effect; he has simply forgotten to shave. His shoulder-length hair – thick, brown and slightly curly – also defies form and shape and falls around his face where it pleases. Similarly, the eclectic ensemble worn loosely on his hard thin frame shows that he doesn't care about clothes or, Tereza suspects, any material possessions. Most of all she is struck by the expression in his black eyes; at once penetrating and other-worldly.

'OK,' Tereza replies. 'I've never finished a relationship before starting it. That's original don't you think?'

Tomas leans back in his chair to listen.

'Last night after we met at the club,' Tereza says, 'I went back to the hotel with my date, an American banker called Hank.' She pauses and decides to continue.

'He'd just closed a big deal, selling a whole lot of shit to some fat Russian guy – can you believe it? He was tanked up on champagne and cocaine, so by the time we got to the hotel, what with his shit deal, the champagne and the cocaine he was buzzing.'

Tomas remains unmoving in his chair.

'So he wants to do this new thing. He gets me to undress and lie spreadeagled on the bed. He strips off and crouches on all fours in front of the bed where he can see me.' Tereza pauses again, continues quickly as if she is about to take medicine and wants to get it over with.

'He pulls out a rasher of bacon and rolls it into a ball, which he ties with a piece of string. He pushes another piece of string through the middle of the ball and makes a knot to hold it. He gives me one end and tells me to pull when he says. He swallows the ball, gags and just stops himself from being sick.'

Tereza's momentum is now unstoppable. Even while speaking she thinks, 'Well, you asked for it.'

'Hank starts to pleasure himself, watching me on the bed. Because he's drunk and wasted, this takes some time. I'm also drunk and I see Hank turn into a pig, then back into Hank, then into a pig again. Hank cum pig, on all fours in front of me, masturbating, with a bacon ball attached to a string down his throat.'

'Eventually he reaches his climax and with an urgent 'Urrgghh' signals me to pull the string. I do it hard. Instantly he vomits. His body contorts from the double sensation of climaxing and vomiting simultaneously. It's revolting. The alternation between Hank and pig stops and only the pig remains.'

'I'm disgusted and pull back. My look is as plain as daylight. The pig takes offence, lunges forward and smashes a trotter across my face. I fall off the bed on to my back, more stunned than hurt. I close my eyes to catch my breath.'

'When I open them there's a pink sphere floating inches above my face. It's the pig's arse. It's squatting over me. Before I have time to move, it relieves itself on me, grunting and snorting. It's over in seconds and there I am on the floor spitting foulness from my mouth. The pig trots off. I hear a door slam and I know it has left.'

Tereza leans forward and using her eyes says, 'How's that for the truth?'

Kaaboom! Tomas's heart is wrung. He begins to shake, his black eyes filling with tears.

'But,' he says, 'you're an angel. A golden angel.'

'No,' Tereza replies, 'I'm not golden, I'm faded grey. And I'm not an angel, I'm a prostitute.'

Things are rarely what they seem . . .

They stare at each other, eyes unspeaking, for a long time. The truth torpedo has scored a direct hit and Tomas is sunk. Tereza decides to launch a rescue mission.

'We've done your experiment. Now I've got a question for you,' she says.

Tomas doesn't reply, verbally or visually.

'What's the difference between a prostitute and a girl who marries for money?'

Tomas remains adrift.

'OK,' Tereza continues, 'let me give you a clue. At the bottom of the chain there's the fifty-euro street hooker. Then come the phone-booth dialup girls. After that are the internet "escorts", and next models who'll be your "friend" for two thousand euros. But the biggest beast in the jungle is the girl who marries for money.'

'There's no difference, then,' Tomas says. 'They're all prostitutes.'

'Wrong,' Tereza replies. 'With a prostitute, you know what you're getting. With the girl who marries for money, you're in trouble.'

'Fine,' says Tomas. 'Prostitution is a nobler profession than gold digging. So what? Most people live normal lives.'

'Do they?' Tereza replies. 'What about all the quick grabbing for happiness, the thoughtless coupling, the selfish and stupid unions, the "Look at me! Look at me on my wedding-day!"? And then what? Disappointment, deception, separation.'

'So it's better to be a prostitute than get divorced?' he asks.

'I'm going to show you a secret,' Tereza replies. 'You can work it out. But first we've got to choose some people.'

Tomas gives a shrug like a child refusing to play.

Tereza looks around the cafe. 'OK. I choose the grandfather sitting over there with his grandson, the Euro couple and the old lady by herself in the corner.'

By now it's getting dark. Tereza guides Tomas along the seafront towards a spit of land at the end of the city. From afar they see the twinkling lights of a funfair. Soon they can hear merry-go-round music.

They walk through the Ferris wheels, shooting galleries and candy-floss stalls. He experiences everything in slow motion, the colours smudged, the music dulled. They sit on a bench at the water's edge. There Tomas in his desolation and Tereza in her fatigue fall asleep.

When they wake, the fairground is closed, the bright lights and tinkling music extinguished. Tereza takes Tomas by the hand and leads him to a spaceship attraction with 'The Ride of Your Life' painted in big letters on its side.

Tereza stops in front of the spaceship and stretches out her arms. Steam billows as a door opens and a beam of light illuminates a ramp on to which she steps. Amazed, Tomas follows.

'This,' she says, 'is a time machine. Here's how it works.' She sits in a pilot seat and signals to Tomas to take the one beside her. Before them is a console of buttons, knobs, levers and a giant screen.

'It's easy to use,' Tereza continues. 'You just plug in what you want to see and the machine does the rest. Look.'

Tomas sees a picture of the grandfather sitting with his grandson in the cafe a few hours earlier. Tereza presses a button and Tomas hears the old man say, 'You know, Ludovicio, all you've got in this world is your honour. This is sacred.'

Tereza moves a dial and a picture of the grandfather as a young man is displayed. He's in an orchard comforting a girl. 'I hate him,' she tells the young man. 'He comes home late every night. Your brother is a drunk and a bum. Sometimes he smells of other women. I can't take it.'

The young man's consoling hand strays to the girl's breast. They lock eyes and he lowers her to the ground.

Tomas looks at Tereza, stunned.

'Press this button and the machine adds some touches of its own,' she says. 'Look, the Euro couple.'

The screen shows them at their first meeting a few years ago. They're at a club, in a crowd that is alive with pleasure. They have sex that night.

A fabulous wedding appears on the screen. The church is decorated with flowers, the congregation magnificent. The ceremony begins. A groomsman a few rows from the back starts playing with his BlackBerry. Soon all the bankers in the congregation are playing with their Black-Berries.

The bride turns to her groom to speak the sacred words. To her horror, he too is playing with a BlackBerry. She spins around, seeking consolation from the congregation, but all the men have turned into hedges, playing Black-Berries with their leafy hands. She tries to remonstrate with her groom but he is now a hedge as well.

A few years later, they see the bride explaining to her children why their father has left home. The children cry.

'Finally,' says Tereza, 'the old lady.'

There she is on screen, a beautiful girl escorted by a smooth-looking type, the sort that plays the cad in an old movie. He's a count with limitless family estates, or so he says. They marry and after years of living a half-life together he dies. But he's not a count, he's a cad. And there aren't estates, only debts.

Worst of all, the waiters whose purpose is to be rude now feel sorry for her. 'Your usual table, countess?' they ask before forgetting to bring the bill.

'You see, Tomas,' Tereza says, 'we all have our stories. At least in mine there are no children crying and all the waiters are rude.'

Tomas looks at her amazed. His eyes are speaking again. 'I love you,' they say.

A modern-day Little Red Riding Hood . . .

A single shot rings out and echoes around the hills. Moments earlier, the pretty girl had been flying in a circle, her father's strong arms holding her aloft and swinging her around. 'You're an angel,' he says, 'you can fly, fly away.'

Now she tumbles hard to the ground, her father slumped beside her. Instantly she enters another world.

This hasn't happened. Her father, the foundation of her life, fallen? He must be playing. A red stain seeps across his shirt. Within seconds it's soaked. The pretty girl's breath comes hard and fast. She squats on all fours like an animal and is violently sick. As she lifts up her head, spittle drooling from her mouth, she sees it on the hillside.

The black wolf puts down his rifle and stands up on his hind legs like a man. He's big, over six foot, with an arched back that bends him forwards. Even from a distance she can see his long snout and snarling mouth, the hideous distended tongue lolling between the fangs. His ears are massive pricked-up triangles and his eyes miniature black beads. As he returns her gaze, he slowly raises his front legs before him like a demon about to cast a spell.

The pretty girl stands up to face her father's murderer. Another random shot, another senseless death in the killing fields around Sarajevo. Now she feels she's slipping from another world into a dream, or rather a nightmare. For the wolf, with exaggerated slowness, arches his shoulders and tilts his snout towards the sky; then he straightens to an upright position, moving one leg forward with an overpronounced step. He repeats this strange manoeuvre, still at a snail's pace, with his front legs outstretched before him like arms, claws clenching and unclenching, eyes fixed on the pretty girl. His intent is clear. He's coming to get her.

The bubble bursts. This isn't another world, a dream or a nightmare. It's death, real and sadistic, carried on slow legs down the hill. The pretty girl runs to her house.

She knows she can't wield her father's revolver, but

perhaps there's another way of using it. Strangely, in this moment of panic and horror, an idea forms. She hauls the gun from the floor and hides it on top of the mattress beneath a sheet.

Through the window she sees the wolf coming; moments later, she hears his howl. The monster is announcing his mission, which is understood all too clearly by the pretty girl. She knows what she must do: she strips naked.

The sound of the front door opening announces the wolf's arrival; seconds later, she hears his claws on the stairs. The beast is now in the doorway, staring at her. This is it. She can faint and die. Or stay conscious and maybe live. With a supernatural effort, she gestures to the wolf to lie on the bed. He will have her anyway. She offers to pleasure him in return for a merciful end.

The wolf lies on his bent back, his coarse legs sticking up stiffly. His grotesque form is nothing compared to his stench. His coat crawls, more putrid than a sewer. The pretty girl only just manages to swallow her bile as her hands fumble for the revolver.

The first shot, fired from the gun lying on its side on the mattress, catches the beast in the thigh. He emits an insane shriek and leaps vertically into the air. As he lands on his back, the second, third and fourth shots perforate his groin. He howls in agony holding his shattered parts and rolls off the bed.

She can kill him now. His head is inches from the gun's mouth and there are two shots left. All she need do is tilt the barrel towards him. Without hesitation, she abandons the gun and runs out of the house.

Days later she's in a bus travelling west, her face, like her heart, set in rock. She'll now do whatever it takes to rise from this mire of blood and horror. But at this moment a single thought rises above the rest in the churning waters of her anguish and despair. A regret more painful than an open wound, that the wolf's agony before death was so short.

And the pretty girl's name? Tereza.

Every hotel has its secrets . . .

Tomas's brain is a soup. He needs time to reflect. On leaving university a few years ago he had no thought beyond getting rich. He joined the money herd in a trance-like plod towards green pastures. The main options were banking, media (dominated by Shit TV), working for a rich Russian or getting involved with football, the last two being one and the same. Shit TV was chosen for the anodyne reasons that he didn't want to cut his hair and he wished to continue his prankster university days for as long as possible.

Now, in his mid twenties, Tomas hears an invisible voice and at last becomes a man. But the transition leaves him confused, a condition not helped by meeting Tereza and taking his trip in the time machine. For the world is more rotten than he thought, and nothing is what it seems.

He sits in the hotel lobby to calm down and recalibrate. 'At least this building,' he thinks, 'an inanimate object, with foundations, rooms and a roof, is what it seems.'

Perhaps if he fixes on a simple physical reality, he can then consider more complex human issues.

There's something laughing at him. It's the invisible voice. 'So you think this hotel is what it seems?' it says.

'Well it's not a dancing elephant,' Tomas replies.

The invisible voice continues to laugh. 'You need some help. I'm going to introduce you to my friend, the invisible eye.' Tomas sits back to await the introduction.

The concierge sees Tomas across the lobby. He has been sitting with no purpose for some time. The concierge comes over to investigate. 'Does Sir need anything?'

'That's very kind,' Tomas replies. 'No, thank you very much.'

But the concierge is unconvinced. He's trained to sense what patrons may want but are unable to say. 'Perhaps Sir would like some companionship?'

Tomas imagines the concierge stripping off his frock coat and cravat to reveal a Hawaiian patterned shirt and shorts underneath. 'Come on, Sir, let's go,' he cries in the voice of a child arriving at a seaside town after a long car journey. They run out of the hotel together laughing. 'Beat you to the ice-cream van, Sir,' the concierge says. But this isn't the companionship on offer.

He waves the concierge away.

'Perhaps later?' the concierge says.

As he returns to the front desk, an overweight businessman in a suit and tie arrives to check in. He's a convention delegate. Although his conference is about to start, he's keen to get to his room. The invisible voice introduces the invisible eye to Tomas who can suddenly see from wherever the eye may be floating. The eye follows the delegate upstairs and sees him fling his shoulder bag on to the bed and head straight for the television. 'These things are so damn difficult to use,' the businessman says to himself.

He presses the 'guest services' button and 'channels' comes up. He scrolls through 'information', 'news', 'sports' and 'kids' and fixes on 'movies'. He presses the 'select' button. He moves the cursor through 'action', 'drama' and 'comedy' and rests it on 'adult'. He pushes 'select'. Before him is a cornucopia of eastern European, Asian and Latino possibilities. His heart begins to race.

He arrives for the conference half an hour late knowing his secretary will smooth over the unidentified 'guest service' on his expenses claim. She understands the need of a grown man on a business trip to watch a fragment of film at two forty-five in the afternoon.

The invisible eye floats through the wall to the room next door. A scruffy-looking traveller has timed his departure well. His minibar has just been checked: he tells the receptionist that he wants his bill in five minutes. He empties the alcoholic contents of the minibar into his carry bag, where the midget bottles jingle against the soaps, sachets of shampoo and other toiletries he has already removed. A hotel blanket is folded on top to cover his shame.

At reception he is asked, 'Has Sir had anything from the minibar?'

'Nothing,' he replies. His bill is printed with a short but impressive whirr. 'So what?' he thinks as he declines the concierge's offer of help with his bag, 'I'm never coming here again.'

The invisible eye continues its spectral progress and sees a pretty undermaid surrender to the embrace of the hotel manager – soon she'll be a full maid; a married man removes his identification mark as a girlfriend opens the bedroom door; a street-corner type, a friend of the concierge, delivers an envelope containing something that is not available on the hotel menu to one of the suites.

'Now for the grand finale,' the invisible voice says to Tomas.

Tomas remains motionless, sitting in the lobby with a view of the hotel bar. It's dusk and the hotel guests are gathering at the watering hole. The invisible eye comes to rest on Tomas's forehead and provides him with a special perspective.

The men are monkeys, chimpanzees and other swinging animals. The girls are storks, stilts and various long-legged birds. As the drinking starts they circle each other cautiously. An orang-utan catches the eye of a flamingo. He 'ooh – oohs', she squawks. Moments later they come together.

A dance starts. An ape begins to waltz with a harrier. A gibbon bows to an ostrich before conducting her to the dance floor. Soon all is a swirl of colours, feathers, beaks and fur. Then the music stops and Tomas sees the animals paired off in separate hotel rooms, missions accomplished.

The concierge distracts Tomas from his reverie. The invisible eye vanishes. 'I feel sure Sir would be interested to make the acquaintance of a most charming young lady.'

Tomas blinks, signifying nothing.

'She's a recent arrival in our little paradise. An exquisite sun-burnished beauty. Adorable. Very popular with the clients. I can arrange an introduction within the hour. Her name is Tereza.'

Ignoring the concierge, Tomas walks out of the hotel into the night. He crosses the street that separates the hotel from the beach and stands on the seaside promenade facing the building. Its magnificent turn-of-the-century facade, with elegant balconies and massive masonry, is lit up by outdoor lamps and moonlight.

He stretches out his arms and focuses on the ornate frontage. Through a window he sees the back of an ape bent between two thin pink legs spread akimbo in the air. On the balcony next door an aging producer is practising his magic arts on a beautiful young producee. Above them is the silhouette of a man in a bathrobe who is introducing himself for the first time to three girls in party dresses.

Tomas concentrates on the rhythm of the hotel: the voices, noises and heartbeats of those inside. He picks up an irregular pulse. Slowly this increases in volume and begins to synchronise into a single beating note. Stretching the palms of his hands upwards, he raises his arms to chest height. The beat doubles in time and volume. A green energy emanates from the hotel like a creeping mist and locks on to his outstretched arms.

He begins to shake. The energy is strong, almost over-powering. The beat rises to a fever pitch. He tilts the palms of his hands downwards and focuses the energy on to the hotel's foundations. There is a deafening roar like a dam bursting and the hotel begins to smoke and vibrate. Tomas's body stiffens as if in shock. He is shaking uncontrollably.

Tomas raises his arms higher and the hotel lifts off the ground with a terrible groan. He clenches his teeth in a spasm of pain and the building rises above its seaside mooring. Tomas is convulsed by a river of sweat; not an inch of his body remains dry. He lets out a scream, like some monstrous thing caught in a pit of horror and despair, and the hotel soars high above the city. It hovers for a moment just beneath the cloud line and then disappears into space.

How to catch a killer . . .

Tomas's morality lessons don't go unnoticed by the Prefect of Police. The first two incidents, although regrettable, don't warrant disturbing his routine. What with his siesta, his mistress and the constant need to adjust his fine prefect's hat, often in the reflection of street windows, the prefect's a busy man. But a large envelope from Boss Olgarv, the fact that the beachside hotel was his favourite clandestine meeting place, and duty, in that order, require the prefect to investigate the disappearance of the hotel.

The loss of the hotel ruins the symmetry of the beachfront; it's as if a front tooth's been wrenched from a mouth. The crater left behind is difficult to explain. The prefect removes his hat to scratch his head.

'Theories, gentlemen?' he asks his squad.

'A madman, prefect,' a detective replies, 'possessed of a technology that extracts all matter leaving only a hole. We must call in the guard, tanks on the streets, sharpshooters, roadblocks, searchlights . . . '

'Thank you, detective,' the prefect says. He replaces his hat and makes a mental note to adjust it at the first opportunity. 'Gentleman, I declare a street carnival,' he announces. His colleagues shuffle their feet, confused. 'Our killer is drawn to people with colour and no purpose. We'll set him a trap. Make the arrangements.'

For the next few days, carnival fever infects the Riviera. Posters at street corners and seaplanes dragging carnival banners in their wake proclaim the arrival of the great day.

But the prefect knows that a little local colour won't be enough to catch his man. He must provide an irresistible target.

As carnival day approaches, word spreads that a famous socialite will be appearing. The press pack froths into a frenzy. While most socialites do rudimentary jobs or good works alongside their socialising, the one promised at the carnival is distinguished above all others. She's famous for nothing. Her uselessness is so pure that it transcends the meaning of the word.

Over the years journalists and detectives have searched high and low for a single meaningful point to her existence; the highest mountains have been climbed, the deepest gorges explored in pursuit of a clue. But not a scintilla of a redeeming feature has been discovered. She is the crowned queen of futility.

The prefect's plan is, however, still more ingenious. While holding his hat, lest the force of his revelation knocks it from his head, he whispers a secret to a favoured paparazzo. The prefect, whose profession it is to know all things, has it on good faith that the socialite, in defiance of all rules of taste and custom, is planning to wear a certain article of under-clothing on carnival night. More daringly still, this sartorial faux pas will become immediately apparent when she steps from her car.

In polite society socialites never wear underclothing. To de-car unexposed is unthinkable. But the socialite's genius transcends these strictures. This is her plan. Let the world prepare.

The slavering press hounds become rabid. Although they're only dogs, they understand the possibilities presented by the planned sartorial mishap. And just as the prefect intended, news of the carnival, the socialite and her unorthodox dressing habits reaches far and wide.

On carnival day the city is quivering with excitement. The army of paparazzi dogs forms a menacing rampart of camera lenses, all six feet long. If a time-travelling Roman legion materialised at this moment, the general in charge would surrender on the spot.

The socialite's car pulls up. A storm of clicks ensues. The driver walks round to the passenger door and touches the handle. The press pack howls, a torrent of saliva despoils the flowery sidewalk. They're no longer dogs, they're wolves and it's a full moon tonight.

The door opens and a giraffe stiletto appears at the edge of the car. A full leg comes into view. This is it. Man's first step on the moon. A star going supernova. The socialite's private area unexposed.

But what's this? A female triangle? A pall of disappointment descends on the pack and they lower their weapons. Now would be a good moment for the time-travelling Romans to attack.

The prefect bustles forward and bundles himself into the car, pushing the socialite back into her seat. 'Mademoiselle, you're correctly undressed. If you'll permit me,' he says.

He removes his hat and holds it at floor level before her. French Prefects of Police never carry fewer than three pairs of female underpants in their caps. He turns to look out of the window. The socialite selects one and the prefect replaces his hat. She emerges once again. Honour is satisfied. The pack is back in business.

Tomas surveys the scene with rising anger. The prefect's right. This is fertile ground for another morality lesson. But there's danger. All that the police interspersed in the crowd need do is wait for the gunman to identify himself, then pounce.

Tomas calculates his attack but something holds him back. His previous sprees, justifiable as they were, now seem to have been so annihilating, so final. Of the magnificent seaside hotel not a brick remains. Tomas wants a momento of his exploits. Even killers can be nostalgic for a souvenir.

He spies the prefect's hat over the sea of heads. It's a fine hat, he thinks. And in the hustle and bustle of the carnival atmosphere it won't be difficult to appropriate and carry away. He approaches from behind and removes the hat with such stealth that it's a full ten seconds before the prefect discovers his loss.

Tomas makes use of this time to leap through the crowd towards freedom. On the point of escape he puts the hat on his head, laughing. But what's this? What's this horror of everything he hates most that permeates his cerebral core? He freezes on the spot.

Within moments he's surrounded by the gendarmerie. It's obvious who he is. The prefect has his man.

The prefect steps through the cordon of officers. The honour of the kill is his. Press and paparazzi now create a second cordon to record the historic moment. 'What will the prefect say?' the cry goes up. 'I arrest you in the name of the law'? 'Killer prepare for justice'? 'Surrender. Prison awaits'?

'My hat if you please, monsieur,' the prefect says.

Jungle law and a difficult question . . .

In every society in each generation there are a few individuals who stand above their peers in intelligence, integrity, decency and strength. Often, in times of war or national tumult, these great people become leaders and shape history; at other times they achieve high status in politics, the arts or sciences and make a lasting contribution.

Judge Reynard is such a man. In his youth he trained as a doctor and mastered general medicine and rudimentary surgery with ease. He excelled particularly in psychohypnosis. But he yearned for a wider role in life and switched to law. After years of distinguished practice he became a judge and finally head of the judicial system.

In this position he made many improvements, big and small, based on the values of reason, fairness and compassion. He retired as one of the country's foremost men.

Tragically for the judge, he now has a wasting disease. While this doesn't affect his mental capacities, it will in due course kill him. But this is some years away. More immediate is the prospect of Tomas's trial. Shit TV has whipped up such a frenzy of fury against its former star that the Supreme Justices can think of only one man to preside over the judicial process. Judge Reynard comes out of retirement to accept this final commission with grace and a certain weary resignation, subject to a number of conditions that he lays down beforehand. He is fatigued not only by age and illness but also by a lifetime's exposure to the legal system.

The first day of the trial arrives and the court crier orders, 'Silence.' Judge Reynard's kindly face appears atop the forest of polished wood over which he presides. He looks frail but his darting eyes, which have seen so much, take in every detail.

In accordance with Reynard's pre-trial conditions, an owl represents Tomas in his defence, the prosecutor is a fox and the jury a battery of hens. Despite his good intentions, Reynard didn't forsee the problem that this presents: throughout the proceedings the fox is unable to concentrate on the issue at hand and his orations are littered with inappropriate similes. 'Judge, you should know that Tomas destroyed the hotel like an animal devouring a roast chicken,' the fox says.

'Kindly explain to me,' Judge Reynard asks, 'why destroying the hotel is like eating a chicken?'

'They both cease to exist, judge,' the fox replies.

This kind of talk is unsettling for the jurors, who decide to keep their heads down and spend the trial knitting cardigans. The hens have no interest in Tomas's adventures and their sole contribution is to emit a congratulatory cluck each time one of their number lays an egg.

The owl is similarly unhelpful. The judge selected this bird on the basis of its reputation for wisdom. But throughout the trial he merely looks around the room wide-eyed, making rapid head movements and dilating his pupils. It seems to Tomas that he wants to eat a mouse, a worthier occupation than randomly collapsing into hysterical laughter, which is the behaviour of the pack of hyenas that occupies the public gallery.

Reynard has to concede that his attempt to interest animals and birds in the law isn't a success. But this, he feels, is as nothing compared to the real problem. Why is it that the law is so slow? Can justice only be done weighed down by a mighty anchor? The judge has spent his career wading knee-deep in muddy fields of cumbersome procedures, long discussions on the precise meaning of a single word, pompous speeches from lawyers seeking to impress. If only everyone would resort to inappropriate chicken similes. If there isn't a better way, surely there must be a faster one.

Reynard knows that to attach a mechanical engine to the wind-powered legal ship of state, judges must have more power. He has no wish for power for himself, rather the opposite; in his twilight years he looks forward to resting unburdened by worldly worries. But judges see so much human behaviour that they can tell, within hours if not minutes, whether a case has merit or an individual has guilt written all over his or her face. There must be a means of making justice swift as well as sure.

With these troubling thoughts in mind, the judge decides to take the unusual step of appropriating all roles – except that of defence, of course, which he gives to Tomas – to himself. He realises that this is impermissible under the rules of law, not to mention unconstitutional and an infringement of Tomas's human rights. It's also likely to invalidate the proceedings and any decision he makes. But over years of practice Reynard has formed a certain view of the judicial system, which now, in this valedictory moment, he wants to challenge. He's also old and distinguished and – who knows? – perhaps the action he takes will set a precedent, always popular with lawyers, or even change the system for good. He turns to speak to Tomas.

'Monsieur,' he says, 'are you content for me to take a somewhat unorthodox approach in these proceedings? I will determine your innocence or guilt and you have my word I'll be both quick and fair.'

'I'd be delighted to submit to your justice, judge,' says Tomas, 'and waive any right to an appeal, on condition that you oblige me by answering a simple question.'

'A most irregular request,' thinks the judge, a smile playing on his lips. But he wants things to be irregular; sometimes systems clogged with the detritus of custom and habit need to be deconstructed in order to be reconstructed better, stronger and faster.

'Proceed,' says the judge. As he speaks, a soft jungle light diffuses the courtroom. Insect song explodes and green shoots appear. An elephant ambles into the court swishing his trunk. He looks thoughtfully at the judge, then raises his tail: thick pats of excrement splatter the floor. The hyenas laugh hysterically. A family of monkeys swings overhead. The voices of a hundred animals echo through the court. 'This is the way it should be,' thinks the judge. 'No more self-serving lawyers. Natural law. Justice in the raw.' He nods to Tomas.

'If you could travel back in time, perhaps by way of a time machine,' says Tomas, 'and assassinate the dictators of the last century who were responsible for millions of deaths, would you?'

There's a furious shriek followed by a symphony of clucking from the jury. The fox has stolen over and put the forehen's thigh in his mouth.

'It's illegal to take life,' the judge says. 'Both according to God and our . . . '

'If you'll forgive me, judge,' Tomas interrupts. 'You're a man of immense lucidity and brilliance. You agreed to consider a question which requires a simple yes or no answer. If a single bullet from the barrel of a gun could save the lives of tens of millions, not to mention averting untold misery and the destruction of property, would you pull the trigger?'

The judge gives a throat-clearing 'harrump' and considers his judicial robe's sleeve.

'Judge, may I be permitted to ask a further question by way of clarification and to help you consider the first?'

The judge gives a silent nod.

'There are a number of men alive today who are without question evil. They brutalise their countries, commit acts of repression and torture, and wallow in stolen riches. The human suffering they cause is incalculable. Were it in your power summarily to execute these men, would you?'

And as the judge again seeks inspiration from his sleeve, jungle drums erupt and a troupe of primitives in grotesque masks gyrates into the court. They leap manically around the room, menacing the occupants with shaking spears and thrusting loins.

'My point, judge,' Tomas shouts above the noise, 'is simple. I cannot claim to be a heroic assassin of evil people in history – although I have recently discovered a time machine and a possibility occurs to me. Neither have I dispensed justice to certain dictators and other evil people, alive today, who deserve not to be. I have, however, provided some morality lessons to a certain class of people who think, act and care only for themselves; whose lives add nothing to the sum of human existence. It may be that these lessons have no effect. Alternatively, it's possible they might be thought-provoking to some. Finally, there's a chance they could result in something good, in which case they may have been worthwhile.'

'Twit-twoo,' the owl says by way of affirmation, and falls off his perch.

THE FRENCH RIVIERA

The magic of modern media . . .

The next day Tereza is sandwiched between a journalist who introduces himself as Pierre and Boss Olgarv in the public gallery in court.

'Haven't you forgotten something?' Tereza asks Pierre. He checks his notepad and pencil behind his ear. He tilts his head to look at his jacket – yes, it's untidy and has a cigarette burn. He feels his shirt collar; the top button's undone and his tie's off centre – again, all fine.

'I'm sure I haven't,' he replies.

Tereza points to his shirt.

'Why, what's the matter?' he thinks. His shirt's creased and bunched up around his protruding belly at the waistband – all as it should be.

'Where's the coffee stain?' says Tereza.

'Damn. I always forget something. I was in such a rush from the socialite story, I forgot to spill coffee on my shirt this morning.'

'That's OK,' says Tereza handing him her eyeliner. Pierre dabs a smudge on his shirt. Close up this looks suspect. But from afar, the view of most people, the mark makes a passable imitation of a coffee stain.

'Forgive the omission, mademoiselle,' says Pierre.

'Think nothing of it,' replies Tereza. 'I'm sure your stories are eloquent.'

'Alas, mademoiselle, eloquence isn't permitted,' replies Pierre. 'Take this story for example – a killer, guided by an invisible voice, attempts to save the world by providing morality lessons to society; he is possibly possessed of a

65

lethal technology or even supernatural powers. It's perfect. I could write pages. But my editor's only interested in socialites and underpants.'

'Oh,' says Tereza. 'And what did you write?'

'I've got it here, if you're interested,' says Pierre, producing the front page of the previous day's newspaper. It features a big colour photograph of the socialite disembarking from her car below the headline 'Socialite – Pants!' An introductory line follows: 'From our reporter at the carnival . . . ' And then the full story – 'The socialite got out of her car. She wore underpants.'

'It's sold millions,' says Pierre.

Tereza still doesn't understand. 'But won't your exposure of Tomas's mind and the myriad sociological issues this case involves delight your readers?'

'Alas, mademoiselle, my art has been reduced to large photographs of thin triangles described by small words,' replies Pierre.

His telephone rings. He answers, holds his hand over the mouthpiece and whispers, 'Excuse me, mademoiselle, it's my editor.' A look of pained concentration comes over his face. 'No, Sir, he's not yet in court,' he says to the disembodied voice. 'Will he be covered in blood and shouting, "Death to socialites"? Presumably not, Sir, prisoners in court are normally clean and not permitted lethal weapons.' He pauses to listen. 'No, Sir, Tomas has said nothing about underpants. Of course, I'll try my best. Goodbye, Sir.'

Pierre sighs and turns to Tereza.

'My editor already has tomorrow's headline,' he says.

'It reads "Socialite and Pants . . . Again!" All I must do is provide a few words to connect Tomas with the socialite's underpants and *voilà* – my editor has his cover.'

'And you have my sympathies,' says Tereza.

'Mademoiselle, you're kind. I would give up smoking for a single good story.'

As if by magic, Pierre's single good story materialises. Boss Olgarv is jealous of his conversation with the pretty lady. Why doesn't she notice something about him and engage him in a discussion? Surely she desires him? All women do. Why, whenever he's dancing on his yacht all the girls crowd around him in a frenzy of excitement.

'Get me the Chief Bear,' he shouts into his mobile. Boss Olgarv has learnt the impressive mobile-phone-call trick. The ensuing conversation, about the 'threat neutralised' and the 'plan proceeding', is ignored by Tereza, who doesn't even glance in his direction, but noted in detail by Pierre. Clearly the Russians are up to something. An article on Russia's new-found militancy forms in his head.

The court crier calls for order and Judge Reynard, looking strained and white, ascends his judicial throne. From this vantage point, his gaze sweeps the court: he notices two brown ears, seemingly detached from any head, sticking up vertically from behind the jury box.

'Good morning, Mr Prosecutor,' the judge says.

The court settles and Judge Reynard raises his hand to speak.

'I regret to inform you that I have some repellent news which goes against every legal principle and shocks me to the core.' Turning to Tomas, he continues. 'A certain media network whose *raison d'être* is vile to any sane person – although not, it seems, to most of the world – has conducted a campaign of hate and vilification against you. Apparently, it is offended by your repudiation of the values it espouses. Disassociating itself from you isn't enough. It has gone a step further.'

The judge pauses, then continues. 'The network has collected a petition of millions of signatures, the force of which appears irresistible. The Supreme Justices have considered the situation and are more concerned about the social disorder that would result from resisting this demand than the implications of capitulation to the network.'

There is a hushed silence in court, disturbed only by the clicking sound of the hens' knitting needles. The owl's pupils dilate.

'In short,' the judge continues, 'the petition seeks your death – televised live on the network, of course. It seems that there is no hope for natural law. We must submit to the magic of modern media. As for me, I was most interested by our discussion yesterday and feel sure that it would have led somewhere. But the matter is out of my hands. I cannot abdicate responsibility for overseeing what now must be: to leave it to someone else would only burden another conscience. I am ill and will die soon. I will therefore expedite this matter as best I can. Tomas, you have my deepest sympathies. Please speak, if you will.'

'That's most gracious of you, judge,' says Tomas. 'May I burden you with a condemned man's request?'

'Of course,' says the judge.

'You will recall my question about perpetrating a small evil to achieve a greater good?' says Tomas.

'I do,' replies the judge.

'Have you yet had an opportunity, judge, to consider whether you would pull the trigger?' Tomas asks.

Judge Reynard wishes to answer according to his conscience. But he's the most senior lawyer in the land; he can give only a sanitised response. However, Reynard is a talented man. He, too, has learned to speak with his eyes. He leans forward across his bench and fixes Tomas with a stare.

'Yes, with joy in my heart,' his eyes say.

Life's lesson learnt at last . . .

'If there's one thing I could bequeath to humanity,' says Tomas, 'it would be a law, rigorously enforced, that once a year everyone in the world should spend one night in a cell imagining they're to be executed in the morning.'

Tomas is alone in his cell the night before the fateful day, trying to squeeze toothpaste from an anorexic tube, with only the invisible voice for company. If at this moment the invisible voice transformed into a visible face, Tomas would note a quizzical look on its brow.

'It wouldn't be a play-acting or token law. There'd also be a drug to induce a "this is the last night of my life" feeling in everyone. People's imagination of their deaths has to be real – if that's possible? After the night is over and the drug has worn off, people realise that they're not going to die. But they can remember exactly how they felt when they thought they were, sitting alone in their cell.'

The invisible voice's imaginary visible face continues to furrow.

'And how's this going to help the world?' the invisible voice asks.

'Since I won't need a toothbrush after tomorrow,' Tomas replies, 'it doesn't matter about toothpaste tonight. At last, a perspective on life. Imagine a world where once a year everyone has a compulsory moment of self-realisation.'

The invisible voice had always wanted to exist, but when this wasn't possible he applied to be a spirit. At least he could materialise every so often to frighten people. But this wasn't to be, either; the invisible voice found himself last in the visible-voice queue. 'I'm sorry,' said his maker. 'There are no more visible voices left, you're going to have to stay invisible. But be quick, the next step down is mute invisible voice.'

The invisible voice knows that because he doesn't exist he of course has a better understanding of life than Tomas. It stands to reason that the best thing for self-realisation is death. When alive, you blunder about confusing trivia with important things, but as Tomas has just discovered, on the brink of death you acquire a new perspective. It's only in death that you truly understand life.

'I wish I could have discussed this with a great man in history,' says Tomas. 'Instead of excreting in Napoleon's tomb, I should have communed with his spirit. What a fool I've been. I wonder whether Tereza's time machine can be used to raise the dead?'

'Of course it can,' says Tereza from the door of the cell. 'There's a special button.'

She comes to sit on the bed with Tomas, making her final visit. She takes his hands in hers. 'But let's not worry about that now. Although you did those things, I know you're a good man, Tomas. Think about that tomorrow,' she says.

'I'm not sure that a good man thinking he's good helps when it comes to dying,' Tomas replies. 'If anything, it's the opposite – he's sad about all the good things he's leaving behind. It's probably easier if you're bad – then you've got no regrets.'

'So what will you think about?' says Tereza.

'That's easy,' Tomas replies. 'Your beautiful face. Dying's easy if you have a single happy thought to fix in your mind. You just keep on thinking it right to the end.'

Russia and the West explained . . .

'Russia's history is written in blood,' begins Pierre's article beneath the headline: 'Russia: The Great Bear Awakes'.

This isn't intended as an insult to the land of Tchaikovsky and Prokofiev, merely a statement of fact. Over the centuries it's been a brutal place. Whereas other nations make war on their neighbours, Russia specialises in slaughtering its own people. From the annihilation of the peasants under the Tsars to the tens of millions killed by the great dictator of the last century. Why is this?

In the largest country on earth, whole areas live in abject backwardness, untouched by the civilising hand of time, let alone television. We scoff at Russian alcoholism and take them for a nation of drunks. But this ignores a harsher truth. The Russian winter is so cold that there's no other way to keep warm. Cut off and freezing, what should the Russian masses resort to – mathematical theorems?

After the victory of the West in the Cold War, the Great Bear retreated to its wintry lair to lick its wounds. But a bear shamed isn't a bear tamed. So what stirs now in the dark forest of the Russian night?

One thing we know. Animals, like people, don't change. The bear born in the wild won't come knocking on the door one day, asking to sit by the fire like a domestic cat. The only means of entry he understands is the sort of force that leaves the door swinging on its hinges.

But force in the twenty-first century lacks subtlety. It's a big thing that can be spotted and squashed. And although animals don't change, they can be trained. What's needed are some new tricks. It seems that the Great Bear has learnt some.

For example, the new Great Bear understands sun-shifting technology. If the sun is melting your butter, why move the butter? Why not the sun? If the Constitution prevents you from continuing in office, why move the Constitution? Why not the country? In the past, Great Bears pawed and mauled. You could hear them from miles away. This one is an altogether more dangerous beast.

The West can react in three ways to the tidal wave of Russian money flooding its shores. First, revulsion: 'Where does this come from? Is that blood? Sorry – we only take American Express.' Second, disdain, the old European way: 'OK, you can come in, but you must stand at the back. And don't speak.' And third, slavish acceptance; the West's actual choice. An avalanche of bankers, jewellers, estate agents and other purveyors of finery, all tripping over themselves to be of service. Why roar yourself hoarse, when all you need do is throw some meat into the arena? Then, you can watch previously virtuous animals make a spectacle of themselves.

Of course, the West had its oversized-collar wearers and dancers with champagne bottles before the Russians arrived. But how much more pendulous are the collars and heavy the bottles now that they're here? What else would you expect? If you're inclined to this behaviour, the arrival of a five-hundred-foot yacht packed with eighteen-year-old 'producees' will have only one effect.

So where does this leave us? And what next? We don't know. But of one thing we can be sure. The winter hibernation is over. The Great Bear is awake and he has a plan. History has taught us that once his paw's in the honey pot, he'll want to eat the hive.

The fateful day . . .

. . . dawns bright and early with a cloudless sky and just a hint of chill in the breeze. It's one of those beautiful Mediterranean dawns where, although the sun's still low in the sky, you can sense the heat ready to explode into the day.

Judge Reynard, as good as his word, takes charge of all the arrangements. As distasteful as it is, he interviews each soldier in the local battalion to select an execution squad of six. He asks each man to consult his conscience, to put aside scruples of honour and duty when considering the matter at hand. To some he says, 'Close your eyes, my son, search your heart.' Shit TV's determined to deliver justice rough, but Reynard attempts to smooth the edges.

After the squad has been selected the judge gives the men a conscience-easing speech. 'Soldiers,' he says. 'Only five of the rifles will be loaded. One will contain a blank. Rifles will be selected at random. Never forget – you could be the man innocent of taking life.'

With the squad in place, Reynard makes meticulous preparations with the doctor in attendance, and a buzzard and a vulture who will take charge of the corpse. These sorry-looking carrion-eaters wear Dickensian top hats with black funeral ribbons hanging from the back. Their long necks jerk constantly; each time they do so their hats fall off.

Tomas is offered a final meal of his choice. He finds this an intriguing prospect. How could someone about to die possibly be hungry or even able to eat? He has heard of executees requesting elaborate final dinners but to what end? It seems incongruous to eat food if you'll be unable to digest it.

He decides to take leave of the invisible voice in his cell.

'Forgive my failure, my invisible friend,' says Tomas. 'What a wasted, thoughtless and money-obsessed life I led before you called me to a higher purpose. But even then I blundered. I thought that eliminating some melting-butter complainers and dancers with champagne bottles, people who exist only to satisfy themselves, would send a message. But my efforts were as chaff in the wind. I ask you though, what could I do? I'm not a Messiah. I have no magic or miracles. And now I'm to die like them, a great nothing: the worst death of all.'

'Don't worry about that,' replies the invisible voice. 'You can try again after you're dead.'

'That's a fine idea,' says Tomas, 'but never having been alive, I fear you don't understand what it is to be dead. After I'm shot, I regret I won't be very good at anything.'

'Nonsense,' says the invisible voice.

Tomas has always been intrigued by the expression 'late for your own funeral'. Partly because it is, of course, impossible. But mostly because he has spent his life challenging the natural order of things, and it appeals to him to attempt to do the same in death. Being late for his own funeral would also facilitate another expression he likes, 'going out with a bang'. At least this much is guaranteed.

Tomas realises that he can't cheat his date with destiny. But he can be late. Playing on the judge's indulgence and the lack of protocol for an execution in Europe in the early twenty-first century, Tomas takes his time to dress and prepare. Without wishing to disavow his recent epiphany on the irrelevance of all things in the face of death, he now misses his toothpaste. He wishes to face his executioners with fresh breath as well as a straight back.

Tomas writes a final note to Tereza. In it he reminds her of the conversation they had at the cafe about the half measures people take in their lives. Tereza used the expression 'quick grabbing for happiness'. Now, on the brink of death, he understands a single simple point – that life is short, too short for compromise. He urges her to take up the sword of his morality lessons where he left off, and suggests Hank as her first pupil.

Meanwhile, the firing squad lingers in the courtyard unsure what to do. No behaviour seems appropriate or inappropriate. A group of four stand talking in hushed voices emitting an occasional forced laugh. Another sits by himself on the steps leading to the barracks, hands clasped, head down in silent thought. The sixth member of the squad stands apart, smoking and looking at the sky. He catches fragments of speech from the large crowd gathered on the other side of the courtyard wall.

Eventually there's a call to order and Tomas emerges from a concealed door. The Shit TV cameras whir into action, every angle covered. Tomas wears a billowing white shirt with puffed-up sleeves, like an olden-day pirate's, with loose black trousers. The bearing of his head and half-smile on his lips betray private triumph. He managed to extract just enough toothpaste from the almost defunct tube to complete his ablutions. He's clean as well as confident.

Tomas is escorted to the courtyard wall. It's one of those fine old terracotta-coloured Mediterranean walls which has seen much use over the centuries. The sergeant offers Tomas the opportunity to speak and a blindfold. He politely declines both.

Tomas straightens his back, legs apart, placing his right foot forward. He clasps his hands behind him, his left hand holding his right wrist. His free palm is held loose, open. He pulls his shoulders back sharply, then slackens them so they come to a comfortable position somewhere between standing to attention and standing at ease. He raises his chin so that his head is pointing up, his eyes over the line of the firing squad. Finally, he lowers his eyes just a fraction, until they are level with the soldiers' heads.

The order to ready the line is given. Tomas takes a deep breath.

'Present!' rings out in the now silent air.

'Aim!'

Tomas thinks of his golden angel and the first moment he saw her, when time stood still.

There's a bang, squawk and furious fluttering of feathers. The buzzard has neck-bobbed his own hat and the vulture's off simultaneously. They flap about in the dust arguing over ownership.

The tension is broken. But Tomas doesn't mind. He was beginning to find the situation pompous. Better for there to be a comic touch at the end.

'Fire!'

TOMAS

The crowd gives a tremendous roar. Millions of network viewers leap up in unison to cheer. And far away in an icy lair the Great Bear smiles silently.

PARIS

3

ILLUSTRATION ON
THIS PAGE

Pigs can fly . . .

A little known fact about pigs is that they can jump. Not high enough to warrant establishing a porcine Olympics, but to an altitude that is quite impressive given the pig's physiognomy and more than sufficient for the purpose Tereza has in mind.

Why, it may be asked, do pigs jump? The answer is simple. Food. The word was invented for them. Given the prospect of food a pig will go to any lengths, including vaulting into the atmosphere, to eat. And what food ensures maximum lift in an airborne pig? Truffles.

Tereza's quest for truffle-jumping pigs involves only a minor detour to Provence on her return to Paris from the Riviera. She strikes a bargain with a local farmer, which includes the provision of a pig-beating staff, and sets off down the motorway with a truck-load of squealing aviators.

On arrival in the capital she meets with an artist friend who has agreed to lend her his studio on the Left Bank. This is attached to a garage via an automatic roller shutter, through which Tereza herds her new friends.

Over the next few days Tereza makes frenzied pre-parations. First, the studio is plastered floor to ceiling with black plastic sheets, creating the impression of the inside of a square dustbin. Next, she installs lava lamps and other psychedelic light effects, transforming the dustbin into a disco for slow dancers. Finally, she hires a motorised builder's hoist with all the accoutrements. The hoist, used mainly for transporting bricks to first-floor level, consists of a platform attached to a mechanical arm, which is operated by an impressive array of levers.

Tereza also acquires a harness similar to the one that was defeated by Boss Olgarv. But Tereza's version is guaranteed by the Japanese cousins of the Teutonic robots. It will perform any task required.

Tereza contacts Shit TV to borrow some equipment and agrees to give the network exclusive rights to the forthcoming show. She despises Shit TV for its role in Tomas's death and regards the network as her mortal foe, but life has taught her to be practical, and she remembers Tomas's lesson that sometimes a small evil leads to a greater good.

Her final task is one of omittance: she doesn't feed the pigs for a week. By the end of it, they are ready to leap to the stars in search of lunch.

With all her arrangements in place, Tereza dials a number.

'That evening – I can think of nothing else,' she says. 'You afforded me the greatest pleasure of my life. I want to pay you back.'

'Where and when?' Hank asks.

Moments later Hank is en route to an urgent meeting on the Left Bank. He telephones his wife from the car. 'I'm working like a dog. Don't wait up.'

When he arrives at the studio, Tereza tells Hank

through the intercom that she's been expecting him. He takes the fateful step through the magic portal. Dancing colours beckon him through an open door at the end of an entrance hall.

Hank's heart begins to race, goes into shock on seeing Tereza.

She is dressed top to toe in a single black plastic garment, which clings to her body like a wet rag. She stands with legs apart, shoulders back and hands glued to her hips. As Hank's eyes adjust to the shifting colours of the pleasure chamber he sees in clear relief the parts of Tereza's body that are exposed through gaps in the outfit. Eyes, nose and the sensual lips peep through slits in the hood; breasts point upwards, forced through two tight openings; in place of a plastic crotch, he can see the triangle of her sex. Were Hank a jumping pig and Tereza a truffle located on the farthest star in the galaxy, he would reach her in one leap.

'Strip,' says Tereza.

Seconds later, Hank is her naked slave, in front of a bank of concealed cameras.

'Lie face down on the platform,' she commands.

He prostrates himself.

Without ceremony, Tereza straps him into the harness. She touches the parts of his body she wants him to lift or move and fixes the straps around his chest, arms and legs. She is meticulous, making minute adjustments on the harness fastenings until his incarceration is complete.

Three words describe Hank now – naked, trussed and prone.

Tereza steps off the platform and swings its mechanical arm, to which is fixed a dangling length of chain, over her victim. She attaches the chain to a loop at the back of the harness and tugs it as hard as she pulled the bacon ball a few weeks earlier. There is no doubt that the harness will hold.

Lying with his head to one side on the platform, Hank attempts to say something. But Tereza doesn't look or listen. With calm concentration she engages the control arm. She flicks a switch and a mechanical noise signifies that the machine is alive. She presses another and Hank rises into the air. When he is chest-high off the ground she presses 'stop'. Hank is left swinging like a caged captive in some medieval contraption.

If Tereza were to be offered her life in exchange for remembering one word of the banalities spoken by Hank at this moment she would lose. She's an avenging angel now, sword unsheathed. Except that her sword is a brush, which she dips into a large pot of truffle oil.

Lying naked and horizontal four feet up in the air, gravity has a predictable effect on Hank's penis, which Tereza proceeds to paint. She gives it several coats, before stepping back to admire her artistry.

Tereza before – dazed, disgusted, sprawled on the floor spitting shit from her mouth. Hank now – ecstatic, euphoric, suspended naked in the air with his genitals coated in truffle oil. Next door a room full of truffle-obsessed jumping pigs, who have eaten nothing for a week.

A demented disco and a rabid raptor . . .

It's the series final of 'Dwarf Slam Disco' on Shit TV and the Great Bear can't be disturbed. Even the Iranian Hawk and Boss Olgarv must wait outside for the show to end.

The scene opens in a cavernous circular arena with brick walls, a wooden floor and dim lighting overhead. A big buzzing crowd is seated in tiered rows running up to a pitched roof. After the American commentator delivers a long introduction, the lights fade and the arena's great entrance portal is flung open. A spectral beam floods the floor as from a spaceship door opening. Instantly music starts to pulse and a huge disco rig descends from the ceiling, flashing in time to the rhythm. This continues for a full five minutes, while the commentator builds the tension further with 'Are you ready?' questions. The crowd starts to chant: 'Slam! Slam! Slam!'

After a while, darting shadows can be seen in the light streaming through the entrance portal. At first these appear indistinct but slowly they take shape and the crowd, straining forward, sees the outline of little mobile figures. And as the music's volume and tempo doubles, a thousand rollerblading dwarves stream into the arena to the crowd's tumultuous applause.

For the next ten minutes the dwarves circulate clock-wise around the space at great speed while the crowd claps in rhythm. As they pass floor-mounted cameras and micro-phones they make menacing faces and nasty noises. These are transmitted to giant screens and speakers suspended overhead: the crowd cheers the more offensive offerings.

TOMAS

The lights fade momentarily, then go out altogether, plunging the arena into darkness. The crowd explodes in a frenzy of excitement and the commentary rises to fever pitch. This is it. Only seconds to go.

An eardrum-bursting klaxon sounds, multi-coloured disco lights ignite, music shakes the walls. The crowd erupts to its feet as the dwarves slam into each other – fists flying, heads butting, legs kicking, teeth biting, elbows shoving: an orgy of pain and violence. From above they resemble a huge catch of fish, just landed, thrashing desperately on a fisherman's deck; a mosaic of a short, brutal, ugly battle. As stretcher bearers carry off the casualties, the mass of rollerbladers is trimmed to a core.

These are the top slammers, two dozen or so in total, expert with their legs and heads. A savage-looking dwarf, with blood streaming from his forehead, pivots on his blade and, incredibly, brings an airborne boot into the face of an opponent. He then swings round to defend against an attacker, arches back as if on a spring, and smashes his forehead into his opponent's nose. The crowd's ecstasy of clapping, cheering and chanting now drowns out the commentary. Ten minutes later just two dwarves are left standing in a pool of mess and blood.

This is the final slam. The dwarves take position at either end of the arena, pawing the floor like bulls about to charge. They snarl, slather and shout abuse. The klaxon sounds and the dwarves take off towards each other at tremendous speed, swinging low on their skates. As they reach the centre, they squat down before leaping high into the air like uncoiled springs. Their foreheads clash with a bone-splintering crunch which echoes in the hall. One little body now lies slumped. The winner is paraded around the arena to ecstactic cheers and applause.

Only now are the Iranian Hawk and Boss Olgarv admitted to the Great Bear's lair. The raptor squawks uncontrollably and flaps about the chamber shitting, his feathers flying. Boss Olgarv manoeuvres his detachable stomach into a corner to watch and listen.

'The pipeline between our two nations is a success,' the Great Bear begins. 'In addition to the technology we've provided and our diplomatic support, you have my thanks.'

The Iranian Hawk flaps over to a table, sending a lamp crashing to the ground. Spooked, he begins thrashing around in circles, squawking dementedly.

'But for the final plan to succeed,' the Great Bear continues, 'the pipeline must be extended. You understand this, don't you?' He pauses awaiting a response. 'It's critical for . . . '

Another squawk cuts him off. Inexplicably, the Iranian Hawk is lying on his back in the middle of the room, flapping his wings and making involuntary head movements. His pupils dilate and his beak opens and closes in short sharp spasms. He appears to be suffering a fit.

'I must stress,' the Great Bear continues calmly, 'that without the extension . . . '

The Iranian Hawk gives an ear-piercing shriek and is airborne once again. The Great Bear signals to his attendants, who roll back the boulder to allow the demented bird to escape.

Boss Olgarv steps from the corner to begin his interview.

'Sir, may I begin with a request?' he asks. 'I'm aware of the pipeline of which you speak but not its extension. Enlighten me a little about the plan. The knowledge will fortify my resolve.'

'Revealing the final plan,' the Great Bear replies, 'is out of the question. But I can put some points into context. As you're aware, our strategy is to subvert the West by flooding it with money. Clearly, the greater the funds at our disposal the more powerful our ability to spread our nihilistic message.'

'I see,' says Boss Olgarv, 'but this only influences a few – the oversized-collar wearers and dancers with champagne bottles.'

'Nonsense,' replies the Great Bear. 'Take football. You yourself own a team. "Ballers", with their vulgar lifestyles, infantile opinions and getting-away-with-it abuse of women, are an excellent symbol of the perversion of values and culture. What young Westerner doesn't dream of becoming a footballer? You think it's the ball he wants?'

'But how are these values to spread?' asks Boss Olgarv. 'How is the money supply to endure?'

'That's my business with the Iranian Hawk,' replies the Great Bear. 'But soon the pipeline will be extended, the venom required to execute the final plan prepared. Your task is to devise a means of spreading it across the West in conjunction with my general, King Rat. A manly weapon, something that borrows from our past but embodies our new virility.'

'A great honour,' replies Boss Olgarv. 'I shall design it personally. A final question, if I may.' He pauses and the Great Bear nods his consent. 'Why was Tomas's liquidation so vital?'

'Tomas was dangerous,' replies the Great Bear. 'A celestial maniac. He understood what was wrong with the world and sensed our plan. He might have ruined it. What if he had started a counter-reaction – an age of reason and moderation? He had to be stopped. Are you certain he's dead?'

'He was shot at point blank range with five bullets,' Boss Olgarv replies.

'Nevertheless, take no chances,' the Great Bear says. 'Send him a death dream.'

Tereza's magic box . . .

Tereza doesn't have the Great Bear's power; hers is of a different sort. Whereas he commands a great army of followers, Tereza presides over a small circle of artists. But thankfully a few scientists exist at the outer reaches of this circle. It's to one of these that she now turns in her hour of need.

The scientist is happy to help Tereza because as well as being a scientist, he's also a man, and as we've seen, Tereza has a certain influence over men. The operation of the scientist's 'box' requires only a brief explanation. Tereza carries it away, along with various electrodes, cables and plug-in things.

She stands before Hank with the 'box'.

'This is a "box",' Tereza announces.

Hank's rapture is now stronger than a hurricane. He looks at the 'box' with wonder, like a child lost in a forest who stumbles upon a house made of chocolate with a Cola pond.

'And this is how it works,' Tereza continues. 'As you can see, there are three screens. The first is red: when illuminated, it shows the word "lie". The middle is orange; it displays "cliché". Finally, green. If this flashes you'll see the word "truth".'

Cables, colours, screens, machines, Hank thinks. A jungle of suggestive possibilities.

'I'm attaching an electrode to your head,' continues Tereza. 'This monitors your brain and classifies your answers lie, cliché or true. For a lie, the "box" lowers you six inches. For a cliché, three inches. For the truth, nothing. The "box" sends a signal to the hoist here and it makes the adjustments.'

Tereza takes a cable attached to the side of the 'box' and plugs it into a socket in the motorised builder's hoist.

'At every lie or cliché, a klaxon sounds,' Tereza adds.

'A game?' Hank asks, a note of caution creeping into his voice.

'Yes, a game,' Tereza replies. 'But not for two players. I've invited some of your friends – or should I say family? – to join us.'

Tereza presses the 'open' button on the control operating the roller shutter that separates the studio from the garage.

There's a thunderous roar like a sudden surge of water,

then a cacophony of oinking, snorting and squealing as a dozen famished would-be aviators stampede into the studio. Their snouts swivel like homing torpedoes to the smell they detect emanating from Hank's genitals.

Hank screams the scream of a man falling from a mountain face to certain death. Spittle flecks his mouth. His chest palpitates out of control. He writhes like a lunatic in a straitjacket, which is now what he is.

'For the love of God, Tereza!' he screams. And Shit TV's audience spikes to a new high.

Birds and a body . . .

The invisible voice can't understand all this fuss about death. This may be because he was never alive. But this, he feels, is beside the point. After Tomas is shot, the doctor checks his pulse. If it's obvious to everyone that he's dead, the invisible voice thinks, why bother?

The buzzard and the vulture flap over to the corpse to perform their grisly duties. The bobbing of their necks disguises their surreptitious sniffs at the cadaver. The initial verdict isn't good. Tomas had been scrupulous in his preparations. Dying clean may have eased Tomas's passage but it does nothing for the appetite of his undertakers. They like their flesh ripe. They'll have to wait.

The firing squad shuffles out of the courtyard, duty discharged. After all the preparation, conscience searching and drama of the moment, that's it. One shot in the morning air and then off to lunch and polishing their boots.

TOMAS

Judge Reynard thanks the squad, fixing each with a stare, and then, head down, departs the set of Shit TV's latest show.

The crowd outside greets the hearse bearing Tomas's corpse with wolf whistles and shouts. They bang angrily on its side shouting insults. Again, the invisible voice is surprised. What do the crowd hope to achieve by this behaviour? For Tomas to hear them and feel contrite? It seems to the invisible voice that the crowd wishes to break open the hearse and desecrate the corpse. Why is it that vengeful crowds in history behave in this way? After someone has died, is it necessary to kill them again?

The buzzard and the vulture pull the zip tight on Tomas's bodybag. The sun is full in the sky, the heat shimmering off the ground. The windows of the hearse are shut against would-be avengers and even in the early-twenty-first century the corpse of an executed criminal isn't provided with air conditioning. All in all, these are perfect conditions for meat to tenderise.

The hearse arrives at the mortuary and the birds trolley the corpse to a room of rest enthusiastically.

The invisible voice notes that no arrangements have been made for the corpse's interment. Judge Reynard, an impeccable overseer of every detail, seems to have neglected this one. Given that the point of funerals is to comfort the living rather than remember the dead, why should Tomas get one? Funerals only happen when people are sad.

All this is good news for the undertakers. They close the door with a satisfying click. This induces an uncontrollable bout of neck bobbing. They clash beaks and heads in their excitement, but they're oblivious to the pain. In a frenzy, they begin a kind of dance, flapping their scrawny wings and jumping up and down on the spot. Tomas, the provider of lethal morality lessons, is laid out in a room of peace, excoriated by two out-of-control carrion eaters.

The vulture eventually calms down and pulls a bundle wrapped in cloth from underneath the trolley. His wings sag under its weight and the buzzard flaps over to help. They lay the bundle down on the table and pull the cord which binds it. The cloth unravels and the buzzard's eyes bulge at the array of saws, knives, hatchets and other jagged-edged things. This is a surgeon's kit from a bygone age. But the buzzard and vulture don't have a medical use in mind.

A fight ensues, as it always does with these birds, over a particularly vicious-looking saw. It resembles a permanently smiling shark and probably has its bite as well. After a scuffle, a compromise is reached. The vulture has the saw, the buzzard a machete which would make a Gurkha proud.

The invisible voice watches these proceedings with rising alarm. Of all his observations today, the one that is causing him the greatest concern is that Tomas isn't dead. But he soon will be.

Drowned in a Russian soup . . .

We dream in life. Well, why can't we dream in death?

In his death dream, Tomas is walking along a seaside promenade on a fine summer's day when a black limousine screams to a halt next to him on the curb. Four burly Russians get out. They are bald, unshaven, with hands like joints of ham. They wear sunglasses and shout loud Russian words to frighten Tomas and encourage each other. He is dragged into the back of the limousine, which makes a screeching U-turn and barrels out of the city.

Eventually they stop in a wooded area some distance behind the city. Tomas is roughly manhandled out of the car. Before him is a large pit, about a mile in diameter and fifty feet deep, which has been dug in a forest clearing. Tomas is thrown into the pit, tethered to a post on its outer rim like an animal.

From his captive position, Tomas sees an enormous metal rod in the middle of the pit. It rises about a hundred feet into the air. Welded on to its surface is a series of bulky hoops from which massive chains run off into the pit. Looking up from his post, Tomas also sees a large concrete structure, which he guesses to be some sort of power station.

Dozens of figures and objects now emerge from the forest and the pit becomes a beehive of activity. This is directed, it seems, by a fat earmuff-wearing Russian with what looks like a detachable stomach, who is standing on the pit's far side. It is Boss Olgarv.

Tomas watches as the figures and objects, all of which appear to be the fat Russian's possessions, are attached to the chains. The larger objects include a seaside villa, a helicopter, a jet and a yacht. Smaller objects fixed to the ends of the chains include a bottle of champagne, a sachet of cocaine, a plasma TV, a jacuzzi and a cigar humidor.

PARIS

Tomas then sees various figures herded into the pit. A blonde trolleying her breasts in front of her, presumably the fat Russian's wife, is attached to a chain. Next to her are tethered half a dozen prostitutes. Beside them is a football team, alongside them some hitmen. Tomas guesses these unfortunates to be the fat Russian's human possessions.

A whistle sounds, there's a humming noise and the ground begins to vibrate. The power station has been activated and energy is surging through a subterranean cable connected to the metal rod.

Slowly, with a groan, it begins to rotate. The massive metal chains holding the people and objects become taut. At first, nothing happens. But as the power surges, the villa, jet and yacht begin to inch along the ground, dragged by the metal chains.

The humans begin a slow walk but the pace soon quickens to a jog as the power is increased and the rod rotates at a faster speed. Within minutes only the football players, who are fit, keep pace with the rotating chains. Eventually even their stamina fails and all the humans and objects are flying around the whirling rod with an incredible velocity.

The fat Russian gives a signal and the power is set to maximum. Tomas covers his ears. The humming is now a single screeching high-pitched note. It's no longer possible to discern champagne bottle, helicopter, prostitute, wife or yacht. It's all just a whirling blur.

Tomas looks down at his feet and notices a yellow liquid collecting in the pit. Within minutes it's up to his waist. For reasons he can't understand, the swirling rod is turning the fat Russian's possessions into a yellow soup. But his incomprehension doesn't matter, because very soon he'll be drowned.

The soup rises to his neck, then his mouth. Tomas shuts it against the liquid and tilts his head back, raising his mouth and nose to give himself precious extra breathing time. He uncovers his ears to free his hands in his struggle against the soup. Instantly his eardrums perforate. Blood trickles down his face and splashes red in the yellow liquid. The rod is now spinning at a speed beyond sound. Tomas screams, feeling his head about to explode. And just as the soup reaches his nose, a cold shock hits his face.

Hank 1: Torture, truffles and truth . . .

If only it were possible to scream your way out of trouble. Despite a bellicose performance, Hank remains suspended naked in a harness, four feet up in the air.

Tereza has calculated, with the help of the pig farmer, that the maximum jump of a ravenous truffle-mad pig is three feet. Just twelve inches separate Hank from an irreversible sex change followed by an excruciating death.

Although Tereza is the architect of Hank's date with destiny she remains courteous and reminds him of the rules.

'Just remember,' she says. 'It's six inches for a lie, three for a cliché and nothing for the truth. There are six questions in all.'

This information, although edifying for Hank, is of no interest to the demented pigs, who continue their leaps unaffected by considerations of truth, cliché or lie. They slather and snarl and attempt to frustrate each other's jumps with nasty bites and butts.

A third party witnessing this scene – the invisible voice? – might speculate whether Hank wants to be put out of his misery. But no death wish can be considered let alone granted, because Tereza hasn't yet had her game.

'The first question is why did you become a banker?'

Hank catches his breath. 'Money,' he gasps. 'It's an obsession. We see magazine covers – CEOs and billionaires – and we want to be like them. To be a banker. It's about status and wealth. There's no thought beyond that.'

The green light displays. A good start.

'And why do you want money?' Tereza asks.

'For security for me and my family. Money gives you freedom and . . . '

The klaxon gives a resounding blast and jolts Hank down nine inches. The lie and cliché screens flash red and orange. The pigs sense that their truffle is at last on the move and redouble their efforts. Tereza stands by impassively.

Hank gives an insane shriek. Just three inches to go. 'OK!' he screams. 'There's no fucking plan, no big idea. It's just about money. We're crazed by it. Our bonuses at Christmas. We just want it – holidays, second homes, first-class flights, stuff. To show off. To have. It's that simple. No charities. No higher calling driving us on. Just stuffing our mouths.'

Hank controls his breathing. He's close to hyperventilating.

ILLUSTRATION ON
THIS PAGE

4

ILLUSTRATION ON
THIS PAGE

'Question three,' says Tereza, 'do bankers give enough away?'

'Are you fucking joking?' replies Hank. He's flying now. 'We fucking give nothing, or only an infinitesimal amount.'

Tereza's impressed by the long word given the circumstances. Perhaps the next version of the 'box' should include a mode which moves torturees up three inches to reward the use of a five-syllable word.

'Yes, there are parties and events,' he continues. 'But it's fig-leaf giving. Conscience relief. A fraction of what we earn. More an excuse to get together and impress.'

The green light flashes. Three questions to go.

'What do you think about big payoffs?' Tereza asks.

'They're fucking great,' Hank laughs. Laughter, like tears, in the face of emasculation. 'You're the CEO. You lose the bank $5 billion. It's time to go. Here's $100 million. And a pat on the back. Good chap.'

Four down. Two to go.

'How do you treat women?'

In cricket there's a concept called a daisy cutter. It's a way of bowling the ball by rolling it slowly along the ground. It's used for children new to the game to break them into connecting bat with ball. Daisy cutters are impossible to miss. And Tereza's just bowled one at Hank.

'At first, respectfully,' he says. 'Can you believe I got married with the best intentions? But drift sets in. When you're working like a maniac you lose perspective. You forget, if you ever knew, your priorities. You start making excuses to work. All-important life-and-death work. You know what I do on the beach with my kids? I fucking BlackBerry.'

Hank's on a roll. There are no rules for a preamble to a full confession, which is what Tereza and, more importantly, the 'box' now require.

'There are a lot of divorces. But even more visits to hookers and strip bars, especially when travelling. What the fuck do you expect? You spend your life in a mad-house, working like a dog, worshipping money. And somehow your home life's meant to be normal?'

The 'box' flashes a resounding green. Hank hangs his head, his energy spent. It's as if he can't go on.

'Take your time over the last one,' says Tereza. 'The "box" can tell if anything's left out. So make your answer full.'

Tereza pauses to let what she's said sink in.

'Apart from now, what's the most frightening experience you've had in your life?' she asks.

The sobering effect of ice . . .

The invisible voice may only be a voice, and invisible at that, but he knows a crisis when he sees one. In a flash he's before his maker.

'Emergency!' he says. 'I need a fifty-foot club-wielding monster to smash into a mortuary.'

His maker looks up from behind his desk with the bored expression of a till person shouting an unenthusiastic 'next'.

'OK,' pleads the invisible voice. 'A giant will do.'

**ILLUSTRATION ON
THIS PAGE**

5

ILLUSTRATION ON
THIS PAGE

'All that's left is a foot in mouth, a blind eye and a visible hand,' says his maker.

Had the invisible voice a heart, it would sink.

'I'll take the hand,' he says. Moments later, he materialises with the visible hand at the seaside cafe where Tereza made her confession to Tomas.

'I'll do the talking,' the invisible voice says. 'You back me up.' The visible hand raises his thumb.

The waiters are, as usual, bunched together at the serving counter ignoring the customers.

'I'm the ghost of the outstretched hand for tips,' intones the invisible voice. 'Do me a service or I'll forever haunt this cafe.' The visible hand hovers in the air, palm outstretched before the waiters.

'Go on,' urges the invisible voice. The visible hand floats off towards the diners. His intent is clear. He's scavenging for tips.

'Stop!' shouts the headwaiter. 'Your service. Name it.'

'A bucket of ice. Immediately,' the invisible voice replies.

Within moments this is produced. The voice and hand materialise outside the door of Tomas's room of rest. 'OK, knock,' the invisible voice commands.

They hear a scuffle the other side of the door. The carrion eaters have been quarrelling about which joint to carve first. A compromise is imminent; the vulture's smiling saw is poised over Tomas's thigh.

'Attention, undertakers,' says the invisible voice. 'Your assistance is required. An experiment in the temporal dis-placement of matter has had mixed results.'

'We're busy,' says the buzzard.

'Hear me out,' the disembodied voice replies and the visible hand gives the door another rap. 'We have successfully transported the entire animal population of the Serengeti to the space outside this building. This is the biggest collection of wild animals in the world.'

'So?' says the vulture.

'Unfortunately, there was a fault with the matter-transfer technology,' the invisible voice replies.

'And?' says the buzzard.

'All the livestock were killed in transit. There are a million dead animals requiring your attention.'

The buzzard and vulture barrel out of the room faster than Boss Olgarv's swirling rod.

'Quick,' says the invisible voice, and seconds later a bucket of ice is poured over the corpse's head.

The second Messiah . . .

News of Tomas's resurrection knocks the socialite with underpants off the front page. In an attempt to recapture lost ground, she strips naked and jumps up and down shouting, 'Look at me! Look at me!' Alas, she's been poorly advised: when nothing is held back, what's left to see? The press pack now pick up the scent of the new story, which they chase with yelps and cries without so much as a sideways glance at her bouncing breasts.

This all goes to prove the old adage 'a good resurrection will always make the front page'. (Or, is it, in fact, a new adage? As far as the press dogs can work out, there's only ever been one resurrection before, also of a man condemned to death, but at a time when there were no front pages.) From the remotest Chinese paddy field to the US President's Oval Office, Tomas's resurrection becomes the biggest media event in world history.

Judge Reynard takes charge and Tomas is transported back to the military base, the place of his execution. There are medical checks, interrogations and psychohypnotic sessions. But what's the point? The truth is clear. Tomas has returned from the dead.

This simple fact is disconcerting to those who shot him. Soldiers are accustomed to straight lines, not supernatural events. If you're shot, you should remain so. To be resurrected is like disobeying an order – unthinkable. The military commander says as much and suggests reconvening the firing squad.

'Is that wise, commander?' says the judge. 'In the few thousand years of man's civilisation only two people have risen from the dead: Jesus Christ and now Tomas. And you wish to shoot him?'

The judge must consult his senior judicial colleagues immediately to discuss the situation but he's apprehensive about leaving the commander in charge. He takes a fateful but necessary decision.

'While I'm away, commander,' he says, 'you're to guard Tomas with your life and follow his instructions in all things. I'm sure you understand.'

The commander salutes and stands to attention. For him, an order is no sooner given than it's obeyed.

Tomas decides to use his new-found powers to test his theory about intelligence and obedience.

'Commander,' he says, 'the battalion will parade at six o'clock in the courtyard.'

Again the commander stands to attention.

'Dressed as ballerinas.'

The commander's face remains impassive without a flicker of concern or surprise.

'The tutus are to be pink. You, of course, are the prima ballerina, so yours will be white and especially ruffled. I'll give further instruction thereafter.'

Tomas has long held the view that it's easier to take orders if you're stupid. Those encumbered with an education tend to be more questioning when told what to do, especially if the orders are venal and pointless – for example, killing other people. Their hearts are just not in it. Others not so burdened do as they're told and get on with the killing. Of course the corollary is that order takers tend to be braver than their more cerebral counterparts. Naturally, there are exceptions to the rule, but in general only the stupidly brave will follow an order to charge a machine-gun nest in broad daylight across a minefield.

The battalion parades at the appointed hour in the uniform specified.

'Half the battalion,' announces Tomas, 'are female swans. You stand to the left. The remainder are swan catchers. You move to the right.'

The battalion ranks shuffle in obedience.

'On my command the female swans will flutter their arms and leap into the air. The swan catchers will give chase with exaggerated dramatic gestures. Commander, you will pirouette around the courtyard, holding the back of your wrist to your forehead as if a tragedy is unfolding before you.'

The soldiers adopt the preparatory ballerina position, heels together with one foot pointing outwards, arms held in front with hands curved.

Tomas gives the command. 'Swans, leap!'

These are battle-hardened soldiers, trained in the deserts of North Africa. To see them leaping and pirouetting, one could easily mistake them for an enthusiastic amateur ballet school, all scoring 'A' for effort.

After the swans have been caught and the commander has given a bravura performance as the vaulting tragic muse, the battalion is dismissed to its barracks. Tomas is left to ruminate on the three points that have defined this historic day.

First, he's alive. How and why he has no idea. Having provided his morality lessons he was caught and in a way tried. Sentenced to death, he faced his executioners with Tereza's beautiful face in mind. He felt nothing but a swirling sensation in his veins, followed by sleep.

Second, the theory's right. The stupid do follow orders and he has the additional satisfaction that yesterday's executioners are today's leaping pink swans.

And third, he now has a battalion of the stupidly brave at his command.

Hank 2: Defining a man's worth . . .

'So what's it going to be?' Tereza asks. 'You're on a plane struck by lightning? Lost in a forest as a child? Ruptured your appendix and almost die?'

Despite the symphony of oinks and squealing, Hank's breathing is now calm. His words when they come are clear and measured. The condemned man on the scaffold making his valedictory speech, untroubled by thoughts of hope or reprieve.

'The night before the big day,' Hank starts, 'sleep is, of course, impossible. But I'd settle for a sleepless night. Instead I sweat like a sick child with a fever; cheeks burning, hair wet.

'In the early hours I drift off for a few minutes, the sort of sleep that comes from exhaustion. I have the nightmare which first came to me when I was ill as a child. I'm orbiting the moon in a spaceship, unable to return to earth. I go round and round, forever trapped in space. I wake up horrified that this dream keeps returning.

'I shower off the sweat and the nightmare but there's no way I can eat breakfast. My stomach is a forest of knots. The thought of food is nauseating, laughable.

'I dress with a crisis of indecision over which tie to wear. Which lucky tie? I choose and tie the knot. My neck swells and I pull at my shirt collar but it makes no difference.

'At work, it's like no other day. It's as if you're on a beach holiday when one day, for no reason, it snows. We

111

all know each other but no one makes eye contact. It's too dangerous. It would give too much away.

'Chuck's called up first. When he returns I pretend not to look but I can't help sneaking a glimpse. There's a half smile on his face, which tells me nothing. Or maybe everything? Or nothing and everything? Who the fuck knows? Chuck sits at his desk and makes a silent phone call to his wife.

'A comic thought pops into my head. Shit TV should screen a series of hushed-voice phone calls, everything people don't want others to hear: whispered secrets; doleful confessions; bad news; excruciating revelations; embarrassing results. It would achieve top ratings. People love other people's pain. The misfortune of others is even more satisfying than your own success.

'I know I'm going to be called up sometime after lunch. But even though I've trained for it, like a sky diver making a jump, I'm not ready. "It's your turn, Hank. Secure your parachute. Jump!" But I'm not jumping. I'm going up in a lift.

'The lift door closes with a finality that says: "This could be your last journey up. Or maybe there'll be more. You'll know in five minutes."

' "Go straight in, Hank," says my boss's secretary. I put my hand on the door handle. I breathe in and out hard. Whatever happens I mustn't show how I feel. This is it. I push the door and go in.

' "Hank, come in," says my boss. "Sit down," and then, "Sit down," again. That's two "Sit downs". Is that as in, "Relax, it's all OK"? Or as in, "I've got some bad news for you, you'd better sit down (twice)"? I sit down.

' "It's been a great year," says my boss. That's an OK start but the words "for you" added at the end would've been better. The first sentence tells you a lot. Maybe everything. I adjust my expectations to my upper-middle level.

' "Your bonus is $3,000,000." That's it. A lightning flash. No preamble beyond the introductory five-word banality. Then three words followed by a number which defines my worth as a man.

'I make a rapid calculation as my boss makes some ceremonial pleasantries. $3,000,000, less forty per cent tax leaves $1,800,000, divided by two for sterling leaves £900,000 net. I wanted £1,000,000 but it's not bad. And the bank's been clever. I'm fed but left hungry for more.

'My boss wraps up and I don't display a flicker of emotion. I say "thank you", shake hands and leave the room.

'I exhale and close my eyes, leaning against the lift on my way down. The show's over. The walls of my world remain intact. But I still maintain the outer pretence. It's my turn to make a half-smile and silent phone call. I can see without looking that the office is watching. They'd pay $1,000 each to hear the secret I whisper to my wife.

'I now relax and think about my £900,000. It's in my account already. One thought warms me like a nip of brandy on a cold day. My boss could've said, "Your bonus is $1,000,000." Finito. Game over. Although I'd dress up my job at a new bank, everyone would know. And then it would be downhill all the way; my misfortune providing pleasure to others.'

Tereza looks at the 'box'. The electrode connected to Hank's head is still in place. Why the delay? Seconds later a light flashes. It's green.

The dangers of deity . . .

'Tomasmania is spreading,' reports Shit TV's news bulletin, 'and all things French are now in fashion. We're hearing of ranchers in Australia demanding delicate sauces with their dinners and Kazakhstani miners scenting their fingertips with Eau pour L'Homme. After two millennia, the new Messiah has arrived. And he's French.'

'This just in,' the bulletin continues. The screen flashes to a picture of the White House lawn. It's thronged with dignitaries, officials and the press pack in the usual sombre dress of those attending a president. A trumpet sounds, but it's not the blast of modern brass. It has the ring of something else – eighteenth-century France. The White House doors fly open and the American President appears, dressed as Louis XIV. He's wearing full court dress of white stockings, billowing skirt and a fabulous brocade jacket. His face is whitened, with rouge spots on each cheek, and he wears a gigantic wig, supported from behind by a servant with a stick. He walks in high-heeled shoes with silver buckles with the decorum of the Sun King himself, making exaggerated gestures. When the camera pans in, he produces a handkerchief from a ruffled sleeve and waves it at the audience.

'The American President has reacted to the craze for all things French and given it a twist. In reality singing shows it's called "making the song your own". People love it.'

Tomas arrives in Paris and, with the help of the judge and his battalion, commandeers a hotel in the Place Vendôme. Where previously a uniformed doorman would greet visitors with a raised hat, Tomas's battalion now guards the hotel with automatic weapons. The soldiers swarm the vicinity, dressed in military fatigues with commemorative pink armbands, to ensure Tomas's total security. Again one might consider the wheel of fortune's rapid turn. From executioners to pink ballerinas and now loyal-unto-death bodyguards. A soldier's heart, once given, is unbiddable. And imagine the prestige of guarding the new Messiah.

Despite the need for security, Tomas slips out of the hotel in disguise to meet Tereza in the Tuilleries gardens nearby. As ever, his heart skips when he sees her. The northern light accentuates the golden aura, which is what Tomas most associates with Tereza. Her simple beauty takes his breath away.

'Well, I was shot, almost eaten and drowned,' Tomas says, as lightly as someone might say, 'I've been shopping and had a coffee.' 'How about you?'

Tereza touches Tomas's face. He's definitely real. But it would be a cliché to interrogate him as the rest of the world is now doing. She's always made a virtue of not following the crowd.

'Hank's a media star,' she says. 'He had an epiphany and confessed the sins of his profession, which our friends at Shit TV happened to televise. And Pierre, whom I met at your trial, has become a celebrated journalist, after having discovered that something is brewing in Russia.'

From golden to avenging angel. He's delighted.

'You need help with what's happened. Pierre can ask questions. He's trained in these matters. I've asked him to join us.'

As they wait for him to arrive, a stranger approaches carrying an umbrella. 'Odd,' thinks Tomas, 'on a sunny day.' Something in the back of his mind triggers a memory; he recognises the stranger's face but the rest of him looks so . . . thin.

Boss Olgarv, minus his detachable stomach, is now parallel with them. As he passes, he jabs the umbrella at Tomas, who jumps out of the way. 'Excuse me,' the Russian says.

Tomas and Tereza look at each other, bemused. They expect him to pass on but instead he turns and jabs at Tomas again. 'Hey!' shouts Tomas, once more avoiding the thrust.

'Excuse me,' Boss Olgarv repeats.

'Watch what you're doing,' says Tomas. But the Russian ignores him and lunges again. This time, he only just misses and Tomas has no choice but to take off at a run.

Tereza watches Tomas being chased around the fountains of the Tuilleries gardens by a strange Russian jabbing an umbrella at him with an apologetic 'Excuse me' after each thrust. The stranger's intention clearly isn't benign; he appears to be a special type of murderer, bizarrely asking for forgiveness after each failed attempt. Although an assassin by profession, perhaps he's polite by nature? Or maybe it's part of his trade? For politeness disarms and can be dangerous.

PARIS

As Pierre arrives in the Tuilleries gardens, a cylindrical object propped up against a wall catches his eye. It's Boss Olgarv's stomach. He stops to investigate and discovers a compartment containing two dart racks – 'truth' and 'death'. There is a 'death' dart missing. Presumably, it is attached to Boss Olgarv's umbrella. Pierre takes two 'truth' darts and hides behind the wall.

Eventually Tomas, who's fit, disappears around a corner and Boss Olgarv, exhausted, comes to retrieve his stomach. As he bends over to clip it in place Pierre sticks a truth dart in his thigh. Once again Boss Olgarv provides material for a story.

Later Pierre meets Tomas and Tereza. Pierre nods awkwardly, unsure of the protocol on meeting a possible deity. He gives Tomas the second 'truth' dart. 'One of these marked "death" was meant for you,' Pierre says.

'Thank you,' says Tomas, putting the dart in his pocket. 'One day I'll use it. But for now I understand you intend to ask some questions on my behalf. Please, if I can be of any help . . . '

'I will of course interrogate your executioners in detail,' Pierre replies, 'but for the moment I'll only trouble you with a few questions, if I may. Do you believe in miracles?'

'I don't,' Tomas replies. 'And I can't explain what's happened. But I do believe in the miracle of ideas. Maybe my corpse was somehow indoctrinated by my beliefs and came back to life.'

Pierre considers the proposition of an ideology so strong that it transcends death.

'I can assure you of one thing,' Pierre says, 'everyone

wants it to be a miracle. The press for their headlines; Shit TV so that they can devise some perverse take on it. The truth is incidental.'

As Tomas ruminates on man's capacity for self-delusion, Pierre asks, 'The incident in the gardens – has anything else strange happened?'

A light goes on in Tomas's head. The umbrella assassin is the yacht-owning Russian who was also in his soup dream.

'This bears close investigation,' says Pierre. 'Whether you're the second Messiah or not, one thing's for sure. The Russians are trying to kill you.'

A beautiful game . . .

Boss Olgarv is depressed. Pierre's second article, 'The Great Bear and the Hawk', leaves him in need of vodka and oblivion.

> Why is the Russian Great Bear such a great friend of the Iranian Hawk's? Is it geographical proximity? Why do these predatory animals hunt together?
>
> We know that the game of international détente is played according to certain rules. For example, you never say what you feel and always calculate what you do. The Great Bear and the Hawk dispense with such niceties. If an individual needs to be eliminated, it is done. Hang the consequences. If a country deserves to be annihilated, say it. Invaded? Do it. To hell with everyone else.

Sharing such martial qualities, it is unsurprising that these allies have established a physical link. I can now reveal that a pipeline exists between these nations, hidden beneath vast deserts and windswept tundra. Its purpose? To carry oil.

The reason for the Great Bear's indulgence of the Hawk's flights of fancy is now clear. It's being fed. While it prefers honey, oil can buy a lot of this.

As we know, the Russian beast is currently flooding the West with sticky stuff; soon we'll all be stuck. The Hawk's pipeline provides an invaluable resource. But what does he receive in return?

Technology, information, knowhow; all with nuclear potential. A launch against the West would mean triumph for the Hawk, disaster for the West and very little to the Great Bear. So let the Hawk have his toys.

Where does this end? Even the biggest honey reservoir will eventually run dry, and the Great Bear needs an ocean to execute his final plan. Read on as we attempt to discover how far and deep the pipeline runs.

Boss Olgarv decides to throw a party to cheer himself up and invites his football team.

But this isn't his only largesse. 'Kick a ball around a field. Here's £100,000 per week.' Imagine the tears of outrage from the player offered only £95,000. 'An insult!' he cries.

Still, perhaps this money mountain creates some greater good? If mansions, cars and diamond ear studs are categorised as such. But the footballer's ultimate trophy is, of course, his wife. In acquiring one, the strict rules of cliché apply: lack of singing talent, trolley-borne breasts and vulgar wedding arrangements are the most important. Detailed sub-rules govern these. Nuptials must be immortalised in the pages of a sponsoring publication. What girl doesn't dream of a six-foot camera lens inches from her nose at the moment she says, 'I do'?

But the rules don't stop there. Miles of forest must be destroyed in the cause of reporting – in photographs for those who can't read – the continuing alliance of two brilliant minds in our glorious culture.

Back to the party, which, like football, is a game of two halves.

The rules for the first are easy and obvious. To get drunk. This is performed as speedily as a pass down the field. That accomplished, the team trots on to the pitch for the second half. At this particular party, it plays flawlessly.

'You up for it?' says a star player to his team mate. 'If you're game?' comes the reply. And then together, 'Come on lads.'

They're sitting with four of their team mates at a table with three girls. One is young – just fifteen – and exquisite. Long black hair framing an oval face; rosebud mouth; soft skin; the lithe body of a dancer: all the prerequisites for a good time. She sits shyly with her eyes cast down, hands on her lap. The star player gives her a cocktail containing his own special ingredient.

'Excuse me, ladies,' says the star player and grabs the fifteen-year-old by the hand. 'You're gorgeous,' he says, champagne breath besmirching her young face. But she doesn't notice the smell. His cocktail is having an instantaneous effect.

The squad moves upstairs with shouts and laughter, carrying the girl in its wake like flotsam. 'In here, darling,' says the squad leader. 'You going to perform for the boys?' She laughs, her head rolling like a rag doll's.

They're in a plush room above the main drinking saloon, dimly lit with deep comfortable sofas. There's a drinks bar stacked with champagne and vodka on ice. The squad charge the bar, like a ball on the pitch, and decapitate several bottles.

'Down in one, sweetheart,' the star player shouts. The teenager obliges, to cat calls and applause. 'Get 'em out! Get 'em out! Get 'em out!' a chorus starts from the terrace of the big sofa, where the footballers are now encamped.

She wobbles to her feet, her world beginning to fade. She's wearing a slip of a black dress. She turns her back to the terrace. This triggers an eruption of shouts and whistles. She slips down her shoulder straps and undoes her bra. When she turns round, she covers her breasts with her hands before suddenly shooting her arms into the air like a fan when a goal is scored.

'Wecchay!' shouts the squad and then, 'Here we go! Here we go! Here we go!' The star player's, 'Come on love,' is drowned out by his team mates' chant, 'All the way! All the way! All the way!'

The girl is centre stage. Six sets of football eyes ravish her. She's the most desirable object on earth. Except she's not on earth, she's floating above it. Who would believe it?

She lets the black dress slip to the floor. Without

decorum, she strips off her pants and stands hands on hips, legs apart, swaying slightly.

The dam bursts. The star player scoops her up and sweeps her on to the sofa. Whilst performing this manoeuvre he loosens his trousers. By the time her back hits the cushions he has penetrated her.

The terrace opposite explodes. This is it, their very own game. 'Go on, give it to her!' 'Take one for the team!' 'Let her have it!' Within minutes the star player is satiated, his semen fouling her adolescent body. He gestures to another player to takes his place.

The girl groans. It's all just lights and colours now. She hardly notices as she's hauled up and turned over, her chin resting on the sofa's arm. As the second member takes his turn, the star player positions a third before her, as if setting up a penalty ball. A chant of, 'Pass it on! Pass it on! Pass it on!' echoes in the air. And then an ear-splitting, 'Weeehay!' as she begins to pleasure the third member simultaneously.

Now it's more than a game. The girl's no longer just a ball being kicked around. She's a cipher for something else, just as the players' machismo shouts and yells disguise a darker desire; one that would shock adoring fans. For the players' eyes now fix on each other's moving parts. By moonlight the vampire awakes. Drunk in the dark, our heroes taste an unspoken pleasure.

The star player now takes up position behind his team mate as if supporting him in the goal mouth. He puts his hands on his mate's hips and rocks him in and out, assisting his gratification. 'Yeah, Yeah, Yeah,' he groans.

Now the star player bends him forwards and, with a tap of his foot, opens his legs. His team mate continues his rhythmic rocking as if being touched in this way is normal. Moments later his tempo is thrown, as the star player penetrates him from behind.

Rapidly the rest of the squad form up, as if executing a manoeuvre on pitch. A player penetrates the star from behind, offering himself in turn to the next member until a pulsing snake takes shape around the sofa, each man moving to a synchronised beat. The fifteen-year-old is no longer centre field: soon she's sent off altogether as the sodomy circle closes. In its dying moments, the game is played in silence, except for deep-throated grunts and groans.

Eventually a collective exhalation of breath, in place of a final whistle, signifies that play is over. The squad zip up with shouts of, 'We gave it to her good,' 'She deserved it,' and, 'That'll teach the dirty bitch.' They stagger back downstairs, leaving the teenage girl comatose on the sofa. It's been a beautiful game.

The future of architecture . . .

Tereza has a surprise for Tomas.

Deities don't usually sneak out of hotels for surprises; they waft about in clouds doing deitific things. But Tomas is a modern Messiah, and soon they're in Tereza's Deux Chevaux on their way to the Bois de Boulogne.

It's late. Tereza parks in a side road. A few moments later, they're at the edge of the park. And there's the surprise. The fairground's in town. Tereza performs her magic trick and they take their places in the time machine.

'You choose,' says Tereza.

Tomas thinks. Oceans of possibilities open before him. The dawn of time? The Stone Age? The Dark Ages? Or maybe the years 3000, 4000 or 5000? He chooses modestly. 'Paris fifteen years from now.'

'OK,' Tereza replies, 'strap in.'

Tereza presses some buttons and adjusts a lever. The machine begins to hum. There's a silent clank as the craft slips its mooring and they glide vertically into the air.

The city looks beautiful twinkling in the night. Tomas is in the clouds on a journey through time with the woman he loves.

'Where to?' Tereza asks.

'Another fairground,' Tomas replies. 'Euro Disney.'

The craft floats above the centre of Paris, which is identical to the one they left only minutes before. The business district and outskirts, however, have been rebuilt – ugly offices replaced by buildings of the same size but in the Parisian style. The workplace has been ennobled.

As they reach the suburbs, Tomas and Tereza are shocked. Paris, always small by global standards, now stretches for miles in every direction. It looks about the size of Tokyo. Yet all the architecture is in the traditional French style with tree-lined avenues, squares, parks and public places.

'This can only mean one thing,' says Tereza.

Tomas looks embarrassed.

They reach their destination. But where's the magic

castle? Has it magicked itself away? On the site of the Haunted House and Space Mountain sits the most beautiful building Tomas and Tereza have ever seen.

The palace is fashioned as a croissant – literally. Most palaces, with their bulky centres and outstretched wings, resemble a croissant to some extent. But this new presidential property has been built as a gigantic replica.

The palace is exquisite. Golden brown, its aura reminds Tomas of Tereza. It falls seamlessly from a high central core to two circling arms with a ribbed exterior. Great curved windows in the roof flood the building with light. A modern Versailles, it makes the original look fussy and old.

In front of the palace, ornamental lawns and fountains fan out on either side of a wide tree-lined boulevard. The craft hovers overhead and Tomas and Tereza gasp at a second wonder.

The boulevard opens on to a space that is dominated by an edifice in the shape of a giant beret. It looks as if it has just been removed from a milliner's box. The rich, textured roof undulates like the creases of the cap; it is a perfect imitation, a million times the size. Like the croissant palace, curved roof windows punch light into its interior. The console of the time machine identifies the royal blue building as the new Parliament of the United States of Europe.

Tereza pulls the craft into a steep climb. Up ahead, down the boulevard that runs from the beret parliament, stands the most magnificent construction of all. It soars three thousand feet into the clouds like a giant standing on a misty mountain top. The three parts of the building, clove shaped, are balanced around a central opening. The largest clove stands upright, occupying half the space. The second, half the size of the first, slants inwards like a billowing sail; the third, the smallest of the three, protrudes outwards at a precarious angle. The cloves are luminescent grey and look like three sculptures in permanent conversation. Seen together, the true form of this administration building now becomes clear to the time travellers – a giant garlic bulb.

'This is how architecture should be,' thinks Tomas. 'Monumental, light, original, patriotic and with a sense of humour.'

Tomas and Tereza are mesmerised. How can France have risen to such heights?

Tomas is clumsy in his wonder and knocks a lever. Instantly the craft lurches with a back-bending jolt and the travellers see a thousand stars in fast motion. There's a bang as if they've hit some space debris. For a moment Tomas thinks he sees two spherical objects with suction pads on the windscreen.

'Hang on,' says Tereza, 'we can reach our time and place. But I can't control the landing spot – there's too much chop. We'll just have to chance it.'

The craft begins to vibrate and Tomas clutches his arm rest. The turbulence worsens. But something else is making it unstable. Tomas looks at Tereza. As her hands move over the knobs and levers, he detects an unfamiliar shadow across her face. Fear? He closes his eyes.

An intelligent show for intelligent people . . .

Pierre begins his investigation of Tomas's Messiahship by trying to locate the vulture and the buzzard. 'Apparently,' says a local witness, 'they've been driven demented by the notion of a lost Serengeti.' Anyway Pierre regards these birds as unreliable witnesses. Would you trust anyone who wanted to eat you?

He then talks to the execution squad of the battalion which Tomas now commands. 'It's as you would expect, monsieur,' the squad's sergeant explains. 'We stood in line. The order was given. We're all expert marksmen. And anyway it was impossible to miss, even if only one rifle had been loaded. We took aim and Tomas was shot, as plain as I'm speaking to you now.'

Next he talks to the smoker in the squad, an uncommunicative man. Perhaps he has been traumatised? Pierre attempts to lighten things up. 'Were I the author of a satirical novel,' he says, 'I could hardly invent anything more ridiculous than the cigarette.'

The soldier carries on smoking.

'All those little boxes containing sticks with big warning signs – "Death", "Cancer", "You will die" – emblazoned on the side. Yet people continue with the habit. It would be the most abstract part of my satire.'

'I know,' replies the soldier, 'but what can I do?'

'Give up, as I did. I made a promise to do so in return for a good story. With the help of a hypnotherapist it was easy. Here, take his number. If you're able to shoot a man, you can give up smoking.'

TOMAS

Pierre rushes off to a meeting with one of Shit TV's top stars. His initial good story on the Great Bear and his disturbing plans for the world has mushroomed into several more; consequently Pierre is now a celebrity and Shit TV want him for their own purpose. Although Pierre has no interest in taking part, journalists are taught to be curious.

The star welcomes Pierre in his black and white office. Everything is black and white, even the staff.

'Hello,' says the star standing up and flashing a smile. 'How nice of you to come.'

Pierre clasps both hands to his eyes and screams, blinded by the smile.

When his sight returns, he's staring point blank at the star's exposed stomach. His platform shoes raise him four feet into the air; he needs long sticks to walk. He's wearing a white shirt inside a black jacket – but what's the point. All the shirt buttons are undone.

The star manoeuvres himself like a stilt walker to a white sofa, where he sits down, propping his sticks against the wall. He pulls the two sides of his shirt still further apart.

'Forgive my sunglasses,' says Pierre. 'My smoking has given me conjunctivitis.' Protected from the perpetual supernova of the star's smile, he sits on the black sofa.

'No problem,' says the star. 'I wear sunglasses all the time but mostly at night. We're interested in you as Paris's up-and-coming investigative journalist,' he continues. 'We're launching a new show that we believe is worthy of your stunning insights and raw intelligence.

It's a retrospective concept, combining several programmes from the past with a new element. One of the contestants has just fallen out and needs to be replaced. There is, however, a small catch.'

'It's kind of you to think of me,' says Pierre. 'But I'm not at all sure. What do I have to do?'

'You're going to love this. You're in a jungle with other contestants, where you perform tasks like eating live bugs, swimming in rivers with crocodiles and putting your head down a snake hole.'

'But that's moronic,' Pierre protests.

'Are you joking?' replies the star. 'To eat a plate of worms requires great powers of concentration, stamina and endurance. This is an intelligent show for intelligent people.'

'Go on,' says Pierre.

'While you're doing these tasks,' the star continues, pulling his trousers up over his stomach, 'a delightful TV chef shouts pleasantries at you.'

'What's the point of that?' asks Pierre.

'It's to encourage the contestants,' replies the star. 'To create positive energy and a happy atmosphere. When your head's in a viper's nest, the chef will be shouting "Are you all right? Can I help you?" with a beautiful cadence.'

'I see,' says Pierre, 'but is there any point to the chef? Shouldn't there be a food element?'

'No, you don't understand; food's irrelevant. Even cooking programmes aren't about food. They're about the chef being nice and wonderfully mannered.'

'So what happens next?' asks Pierre.

'OK,' replies the star, pulling his trousers right up to his armpits. 'Now picture the scene. All the contestants have done their tasks and are covered in filth. You form a line in the jungle and the chef walks up and down shouting, "I do hope you're OK," inches from your face.'

'Suddenly I appear out of nowhere and referee a singing competition, the rules of which are that you must make as big a fool of yourself as possible. The more clichéd, awful and talentless you are, the better you do. The viewers then vote for someone to take a shot at the top prize, taking delight in the knowledge that the recipient will never be heard of again and spend the rest of his or her life a crushed soul.'

'And how do you win the top prize?' asks Pierre.

'There are two steps,' replies the star.

'Which are?'

'Isn't step one obvious?' replies the star. 'What do you think the delightful TV chef is there for? Eat his shit.'

'And step two?' asks Pierre dumfounded.

'Surely you can guess?' the star replies, surprised.

'Eat your own shit?' suggests Pierre.

'That's disgusting!' says the star. 'Eat yourself. Not a vital organ, but a toe, finger or slice of flesh. The more you eat – we're hoping for a leg for a man and a breast for a woman – the bigger the prize. Of course an anaesthetic will be used for the amputation and the body part you choose will be cooked any way you wish by the chef.'

'So let me get this right,' says Pierre. 'I'm to participate in a slug-eating competition in the jungle, overseen by a polite chef, culminating in an abusive game that poses as a singing competition. And if I win I get to eat the chef's shit, followed by one of my body parts cooked in front of me, with a guarantee that I will be depressed for the rest of my life?'

'That's right,' says the star, pulling his trousers to just below his chin.

'And what's the catch ?' Pierre asks, stupefied by the conversation.

'Oh – you have to pass yourself off as a teenage girl,' the star replies.

'What?' says Pierre.

'Yes, the contestant who's fallen out is an eighteen-year-old soap star, so we need to replace her.'

'But look at me. I'm an overweight journalist in my mid forties. How could I possibly pass for a teenage soap queen?' Pierre asks, exasperated.

'Oh, don't worry about that,' says the star. 'Our audience is intelligent but not that intelligent. Think it over.'

As Pierre leaves the office he hears a yell from the white sofa. It is reported later that the star pulled his trousers over his mouth and asphyxiated himself.

In the dark with something scary . . .

Sometimes, in the dark, it's difficult to tell whether you're alive or dead. If you're in pain, you're probably alive – unless hell exists. Otherwise, the trick is to find the nearest light. This provides a beacon of hope until programming can be resumed. For Tomas and Tereza this is a red flash on the dead control panel before them.

TOMAS

There's no protocol for the evacuation of a crashed time machine; so Tomas and Tereza follow custom and instinct. Although there's no danger of combustion, the time travellers decraft. Perhaps the problem is best solved standing up.

And it is a problem. For as their eyes adjust to the enveloping gloom they realise that they appear to be trapped. In a tomb.

Action-movie makers like to put the hero in an impossible situation. Just as you think things can't get worse, the director twists the knife. Suspended on a rope above a ravine, the hero looks down. What does he see? Crocodiles!

But Tomas and Tereza can't see, they can only hear. The sound chills their bones. It is the squelch of tentacles on a marble floor.

Moonbeams stream in through windows beneath a dome. Tomas puts a protective arm around Tereza but neither the illumination nor the embrace helps. The sound is getting louder and coming closer.

'Who's there?' Tomas's voice rings in the air.

Although a possible deity, Tomas still has human frailties. The question is as futile for him as it is helpful to the approaching menace. He has now provided his co-ordinates in the dark.

Tereza tightens her hold on Tomas. The squelching stops and they inch around the side of the craft. The moon comes out fully, flooding their sepulchral surroundings. There before them, illuminated by a beam, is the squelch maker. It's tall, round and looking at them.

PARIS

'Shit,' mutters the second Messiah. Tomas's deitific word hangs in the air. The Alien squelches a step forward and smiles. This only helps a little: is the human smile recognised as a sign of friendship across the Galaxy? For all Tomas knows, the alien equivalent is a prelude to a ray-gun attack.

Tomas shows his mettle as a man, if not a deity, and approaches the Alien.

The Alien is seven feet tall to Tomas's six and is entirely round. Round head, round trunk, round arms, round legs. His eyes are two big spheres, which blink continuously like the owl's at Tomas's trial; his arms, with their three-fingered hands, stretch down to his round knees. Circular suction pads at the end of the spherical feet that Tomas had noticed on the craft's screen account for the squelching sound. The Alien, clad in a silver suit that might be considered fashionable on earth, now raises a pad in salutation. His round-mouthed smile widens.

Although they can't be sure, Tomas and Tereza are flooded with relief. Aliens come in all shapes and sizes – but this one seems friendly.

'We must have picked him up when we bumped the lever,' says Tereza. 'God knows how many galaxies we travelled through. He was probably just out for a walk. I feel sorry for him.'

As the echo of her words fades in the tomb, the most extraordinary thing happens – the Alien rotates. Very fast, in the wink of an eye, he twirls on the spot, smile fixed, eyes blinking. Thirty seconds later the same thing happens. And again. Every thirty seconds, a mini whirlwind.

Further enquiry into this circular rotating curiosity must wait: the more pressing matter is how to prevent this tomb from becoming their own. Tomas gestures to the Alien to remain where he is and takes Tereza by the hand to explore their prison.

Off the chamber beneath the impressive dome radiate chapels. Tomas reads the names – La Salle, Duroc – of two of the tomb's inhabitants. Rounding a corner he sees another – Gratien – and then a monument representing sentinels guarding the body of their leader, Bugeaud. By the banners and martial symbols Tomas deduces that this isn't an ordinary tomb but a military one. It houses the bones of the fallen brave.

Moving farther he discovers a Joseph and then a Jerome. Moments later he connects the names.

'I can't believe this,' he says to Tereza. 'Do you know who was served by Bugeaud and Duroc? The man Gratien and La Salle fought beside? Whose brothers were Joseph and Jerome?'

Tereza gives him a blank stare.

'We can only be in one place,' Tomas says. 'Napoleon's tomb.'

Hank 3: The marooned man's flare . . .

What's this fascination we have with fallen people? The convicted fraudster walks into a restaurant to be greeted by bowing waiters and a reverential silence. The drug-addict singer with foul manners is cheered in the street. The impeached president leaves office to applause and a waving crowd. Is it the thrill of proximity to something bad or the wish to taste it ourselves?

Hank's fall from grace has a predictable consequence. He's a hero. His confession turns him into a repository of wisdom on all things business and banking. Now he stands in the conference room of his bank, to answer questions from his admiring peers. He deals with the basics first.

'How should you dress for success?' asks an enthusiastic young banker, who is wearing a yellow tie and red braces.

'Not like you,' Hank replies, 'people see you coming. You're saying too much. White or blue shirt. Blue or grey trousers. Blue tie. Even a fancy watch gives you away.'

'So once I look the part,' says the banker, trying to cover his embarrassment with another question, 'what attitude do I take? Tough? Direct? Listening? Subtle?'

'Anyone with just one gear's a loser,' Hank replies, 'especially the always-tough boss. That's the ultimate cliché. Worse, it's predictable. You've got to adjust to every situation. If the other side's aggressive, shut up. It can disarm. Don't get into a shouting match – it leads nowhere. If you know what you want, play the tough guy. If you're not sure, dissemble. Sometimes crack a joke. Other times play dumb.'

'Then it's OK to lie?' another banker asks.

Hank pauses. The reconstructed man needn't hold back. He wallows in his candour.

'Truth in business today isn't absolute. It's not a question of truth or lie. Right or wrong. Truth is elastic. It bends.'

'Give us an example,' asks the same questioner.

'A deal has become expensive,' Hank replies, 'you need to pile on more debt to get it done. What do you do? Advise your client not to go ahead? Then what happens to your bonus? So you don't lie. But you don't exactly shout "Stop!" Remember, it's your job to do deals. You tell me: how many have you done that didn't work out for your clients?'

'But that's not illegal,' says the questioner. 'It's not wrong.'

'Like a grown man sitting all day in front of a bank of screens, all to the end of making money for himself. Better not to think about right or wrong.'

'OK, once you've got your dress straight and learned the subtleties of truth,' asks another questioner, 'what's the biggest weakness to look for in the other side?'

'Bullshitting about money,' Hank replies almost before he's finished the question. 'Like trying to fuck girls by showing off about your car or bonus. Only losers slip money messages into the conversation, whether it's business or personal. They're usually lying, anyway. It's the biggest sign of weakness. Strong guys never mention money.'

'And the biggest killer?'

'Not taking risks. You can read every business cliché about setting goals, hiring the best, striving for excellence. But at the end of the day it's all about taking risks, the bigger the better. Even if you fail. Everyone's the same. You've got to be different. "Me too" people die. Risk takers survive.'

'And how do you do that?'

'Go mad,' Hank says, shaking his head like a lunatic.

'Think beyond your wildest dreams. Take your ideas to a crazy place. Then pan back to something more realistic. I guarantee you'll have pushed your thinking further.'

'And how does that apply to us bankers?' asks the chief banker, who sold Boss Olgarv the slaughterhouse business.

'It doesn't,' Hank replies. 'We think we take risks but we don't. Or rather can't. It's not our money. What's the worst thing that can happen to a banker? He gets fired for making a mistake. And to a risk taker? He goes bust or loses his house. We're not in the arena covered in filth, sweat and blood. We're the pond dwellers. The ones who feed off other people's bits. We're there to organise the show, then sit back and watch.'

'Come on, Hank,' says the chief banker. 'We're better than that. We also give back. What about the charity events we hold? And the good causes we work with?'

'Boom or bust bankers worldwide earn vast sums,' Hank replies. 'We give only the tiniest amount and its not systematic.'

'So what are you suggesting,' asks another questioner, 'that bankers should tithe?'

'That's exactly what I'm saying,' Hank replies. 'Imagine what that money together with our work ethic could achieve. Just think if each bank adopted a charity, school or hospital, and it became part of our daily business to support that institution; to use our skills to make it a centre of excellence. Once we succeeded with one we'd move on to another. Think of the public reaction. We'd go from being pariahs to philanthropists overnight.'

'That's idealistic,' the chief banker replies; 'there are always issues, local politics, complexities.'

'Nothing compared to the deals we do,' Hank replies. 'Within a decade, we could become the most powerful lobby in the world. Our enterprise skills could focus on difficult areas, eradicate problems. We're capable of making a difference in whole sectors, on a national scale. Why should we do it just as bankers, to grab money for ourselves? Why not do it as philanthropists and influencers? We have the talent but not the will.'

'Our job's finance, not management,' another banker says.

'Why not?' says Hank. 'Finance; ideas; organisation: it's all the same. Take a small-sized African country whose GDP is less than the average bank's profits. It's corrupt, inefficient and has a myriad of social and political troubles. But there is potential in its resources, geographic position and people. The bank, which has thousands of bankers, assigns just a few hundred to work full time for this country. The problems are enormous, the corruption intractable, but the bank uses its power, influence and know-how to make a difference. It might take years, but in the end there would be a result.'

Hank pauses, reflecting on the apparent impossibility of his message.

'In history,' he continues, 'bankers ran whole countries or communities: the Medici in Florence; the financiers in Venice. Their motivation was just as much civic as it was commercial; they built fabulous cities and endowed schools, hospitals and charities that still endure today. We live in a fast, ruthless, money-mad world. We need to return to these values; to a mindset where the banking class systematically thinks and acts like the financiers of old. Our epitaph will be: they were great bankers, made money and lived happy lives, all while doing incredible things for others.'

'It'll never happen, Hank,' says the chief banker. 'The days of bankers behaving like that are over. Anyway, you sound moralising and quaint.'

'Maybe you're right,' Hank replies. 'But sometimes the best that you can do in life is send up a flare, like the man marooned. However remote the island, someone might just see its light in the sky.'

The greatest Frenchman of all time . . .

The Emperor Napoleon lies in the tomb of Les Invalides in the middle of Paris, surrounded by his generals and brothers. His body is interred in an elaborate encasement of six coffins built from different materials, including mahogany, ebony and oak, one inside the other. The outer coffin, of red porphyry, sits on a green granite pedestal surrounded by twelve statues of victory under a window-lit dome.

Tomas and Tereza walk around the magnificent sarco-phagus and Tomas touches its lip in awe.

'The night before my execution,' he says, 'I found a perspective on life at last. It was my dying wish to discuss it with a great man in history.' He pauses before continuing. 'You said your machine could raise the dead.'

'It could,' she replies, 'but I'm not sure after the crash. The button you need is the red one on the console that's still lit.'

'This is the greatest opportunity of my life,' Tomas says. 'We must try.'

Tereza considers the proposition. 'I understand,' she says, 'but let's practise on his brothers and generals. If Napoleon is to return it must be in one piece.'

Tomas and Tereza go back to the machine, followed by the Alien. In the crisis of thinking themselves entombed, they'd almost forgotten him. Now he squelches along behind them, twirling like a happy puppy.

Tereza enters the names – Bugeaud, Duroc, Gratien, La Salle, Joseph and Jerome – into the console and gives Tomas the honour of pushing the red button. They hurry back to the domed area with the Alien in tow.

Nothing happens. The tomb is dark and silent. At intervals light beams illuminate the scene as clouds pass from the moon's surface. Tomas's face creases in concentration and then disappointment. A clumsy slip has cheated him of his date with destiny. The Alien senses the atmosphere and squelches over to them in solidarity.

Above the sound of tentacles on marble, sharper noises echo in the shadows: of boots, jangling spurs and swords. And moments later six figures, impeccable in full military dress, emerge from the darkness and stand in a semi-circle before them.

The scene is set. Four Napoleonic generals, his two imperial brothers, the second Messiah, a prostitute and an alien.

The two parties stare at each other in wonder. Decorum quickly prevails as Duroc advances a step and bows to Tereza. 'Good evening, mademoiselle,' he says. His comrades follow. Then they click their heels in unison and nod politely to Tomas and the Alien. 'Messieurs,' they say.

'If you'll forgive me,' asks La Salle, bowing his head again, 'to what do we owe this pleasure?'

'With your permission, I wish to speak to the Emperor,' Tomas replies.

'Monsieur, we are but shades,' La Salle replies. 'Our permission is not required. But perhaps we may assist?'

'Of course,' Tomas says.

'If you will excuse us,' La Salle replies and the six comrades form a speaking circle. The men confer in loud whispers; Tomas and Tereza hear snatches of French, punctuated by loud exclamations of disagreement.

'Mademoiselle, messieurs,' Duroc bows again. 'If the Emperor is to awake, etiquette must be observed. We suggest trumpets and drums.'

'All trumpets and drums,' Gratien interjects.

'If you'll forgive us,' Duroc continues. 'I recommend a band of musicians. General Gratien suggests every trumpet and drum that ever accompanied the Emperor.'

'*C'est l'Empereur,*' Gratien adds.

'Gentlemen, please decide,' Tomas replies. 'We're at your service.'

Tomas looks nervously at Tereza as the comrades again join in debate. After a further round of French exclamations they about-face.

'The vote is for all,' Gratien announces. 'If you would be so kind.'

'Of course, general,' Tomas replies, then under his breath to Tereza, 'Is it possible?'

'Why not?' she says. 'I'll just plug them all in.'

Soon the tomb begins to vibrate like the floor of a valley about to flood. Two thousand marching men emerge in formation from the shadows, in every colour and design of Napoleonic uniform, trumpets and drums at the ready.

Duroc takes command. 'Drum major,' he orders. 'Drummers to the left of the Emperor. Trumpeters to the right. A full drum roll if you please. Then a voluntary. On my order.'

The tomb echoes to an army of musicians taking up position around the Emperor's coffin with effortless speed and discipline.

'Drum major,' Duroc says, and nods his head.

The silence is total: not a shuffle, cough or splutter. The drum major raises his arm. A thousand drummers await his command. The drum roll is unlike any other sound on earth; more powerful than an ocean of crashing waves, more electrifying than the loudest Chinese fireworks. A nod to the trumpeters: a thousand instruments are lifted to moistened lips. He brings down his arm. The voluntary is ear splitting but majestic. It could be announcing the arrival of God himself.

The drum major beats time with stern concentration and not a flicker of emotion. The generals, for all their battle-hardened demeanour, disgrace themselves. They cry.

Rivers of tears stream on to the marble floor of the mausoleum. Keeping a straight back at this moment is more difficult than fighting the fiercest battle.

Eventually the drum major raises his arms high to signal the final crescendo. Trumpets and drums join in a deafening blast of salutation. Just as the last note fades in the air, the tomb is plunged into darkness. A cloud covers the moon's face and two thousand souls stand silent in a black abyss.

Seconds later, the brightest moonbeam ever to shine over Paris streams through one of the dome windows. Like a searchlight, painful to the eyes, it picks out a solitary figure in the surrounding darkness. Standing on top of the sarcophagus, head bowed, legs apart, hands clasped behind his back, is the greatest Frenchman of all time. The Emperor Napoleon.

A nasty surprise in a water glass . . .

For days after the football party the fifteen-year-old girl is violently sick. But her fever and screams in the night disguise a metamorphosis. The cub has become a lioness.

She makes a plan with the help of her sister, a trainee nurse, and telephones the star player.

'How about a game of doctors and nurses?' she says. 'I'll bring a friend.'

She has chosen wisely. He likes the thought of playing doctor. In the medicine world, the doctor is king. He gives her a time and place.

The girls arrive and knock on his hotel door. His

pulse begins to race as they slip off their coats. Real nurses' uniforms. They're carrying a suitcase packed with medical toys, borrowed from the trainee's hospital, to help his operation. They lower his trousers so treatment can begin. As they slip to the floor he feels a sharp pain in his thigh. His cry lasts a second, then he hits the carpet cold.

What the girls lack in physical strength, they make up for in determination. They drag him up on to the bed. The suitcase is opened to reveal an array of instruments and drugs, including a saline drip. The girls intend to teach him a lesson, not commit murder, so the patient must be hydrated at all times. A vein is found and the saline tube inserted. The trainee nurse then fills a syringe with a more potent sedative. While she's no expert in anaesthetics, she knows enough to administer the drug in more or less the correct quantities and place.

A plastic sheet is slipped underneath the patient, he is stripped and his genitals are shaved. A haze of disinfectant wafts in the air as they swab him several times. Next the trainee attaches a tourniquet to the top of his scrotum and screws it tight. The blood-deprived area begins to turn puce. Bandages, swabs and cotton balls are at hand. All is ready. The lioness advances on her prey but is held back by her sister. She's the one with the basic expertise, after all. But not much is required. A few flicks of the scalpel deprives the star footballer of the ammunition for his assault weapon.

The blood loss is light and an antibiotic is introduced into the saline drip. The wound is stitched, the patient's

temperature taken; he is given a dose of morphine intra-
venously. All that remains is for the girls to pack up, which
they do in minutes, hooking the saline drip to the bed-
head. The whole operation has taken less than an hour.

The star player sleeps deeply but wakes at dawn. His
mouth is parched and he thinks of the water on the side
table. There's a dull ache between his legs, the cause of
which he doesn't understand. It becomes clear when he
reaches for the glass beside him.

An audience with the Emperor . . .

The Emperor raises his head and looks around in the
sepulchral gloom. Two thousand boots snap to attention.
The stamp of feet echoes through the air. Then silence.
The Emperor's eyes adjust to the light and he takes in
the situation. With a sudden sweep he removes his hat.
'Mademoiselle,' he says and bows slightly. Tereza, woman
of the street, avenging angel, is paid homage by France's
most famous hero.

'Gentlemen, good evening,' Napoleon says. 'I am over-
joyed to see you.' The tension breaks and the Emperor is
borne in the air to cries and cheers of 'Vive l'Empereur!' He
embraces his brothers and shakes hands with the generals,
fixing each with an eagle's stare. 'Come,' he motions to
Tomas, and two chairs appear by his coffin's side. Napoleon
sits with his army at his back; Tomas with Tereza's hand
resting lightly on his shoulder and the Alien twirling to the
rear. The same moonbeam still illuminates the scene.

'Emperor,' Tomas begins, 'ever since my conversion in

your tomb, it has been my greatest ambition to hear you speak about what defined you as a man: the guiding force behind your achievement; the inspiration of your life.'

'No,' replies the Emperor. Not a man moves, except Tomas, who shifts in his chair uneasily, with creeping embarrassment.

'Might it be possible, Sir,' he continues, 'to say a few words on the philosophy that shaped your glory, and the heroic principles from which we can learn?'

'No,' Napoleon repeats. Tereza's hand tightens on Tomas's shoulder in a comforting squeeze. The Alien squelches forward a step. He too supports Tomas in this, the most excruciating moment in history.

'Forgive me . . . ' Tomas continues.

Napoleon raises a hand and cuts him off. 'I can tell you in a word.'

A look of relief floods Tomas's face. He may not be offering a speech, but the Emperor is at least engaged. He leans forward eagerly.

The Emperor pauses. 'Failure,' Napoleon says.

'Excuse me?' Tomas queries.

'Failure,' the Emperor repeats, 'it's the defining word of my success.'

'I don't understand,' Tomas says.

'Do you recall,' Napoleon asks, 'the night before your execution, when you had no need of toothpaste?'

'I do,' Tomas replies.

'Why was that?' Napoleon asks.

'Because at last I had a perspective on life. Facing death in the morning, I understood the difference between the important and the trivial, and I lamented so much time wasted on nonsense.'

'That's correct,' Napoleon replies. 'A worthy sentiment, but felt only hours before your death. You see, I was fortunate to be born with it.'

'But what of your glories, the victories and riches?' Tomas asks.

'Immaterial and incidental. Why should I care about these things? Are they with me now? Do you suppose I hover above my tomb each day and rejoice in what I no longer have? I'm dead. Because I reached a point of self-realisation early in life, I put aside irrelevances.'

'But man needs security, achievement and wealth,' Tomas says.

'Does he? Is this what you're taught at school – to join a bank or serve a rich Russian? Do men need these things? Or do only the thoughtless herd-followers crave them? There are two sorts of men, my friend: those who seek riches and glory, and the others. The former will, no doubt, find what they seek, in varying degrees. So? They die. What imprint do they leave? Nothing. Only echoes. The others seek a higher purpose: to make a difference to those around them; to change, shape or improve things, if only to a small extent.'

'But can't the wealth and glory seekers do this as well?' Tomas asks.

'Yes,' Napoleon replies, 'but never to achieve greatness. They're constrained by their needs, unable to take the risks that define the life of a great man.'

'But we all take risks,' Tomas says.

'Do we? Define the risk taker.'

Tomas pauses to think. 'Strong and brave,' he replies.

'You may as well add "foolish",' Napoleon says. 'No, the risk taker is defined by one idea only, burned into his soul: a willingness to fail. That's why wealth and glory seekers can't qualify. They may take risks but only up to a point. And they would never endanger their spoils or glory.'

'And failure?' asks Tomas. 'Is that glorious?'

'Like death,' Napoleon replies. 'If you take risks, by definition you'll fail. Of course there'll be successes but also reversals, perhaps many. You may even end in failure. I took so many risks that my failure was inevitable. Do you think I didn't know that? I'm surprised at how you perceive failure. It should be celebrated.'

'So you're saying that in failure you succeed?'

'Of course. Look at me in this glorious tomb, the central point of this city, surrounded by my brothers and comrades in arms. I'm the happiest man dead there is.'

'And what did these failures achieve?' Tomas asks.

Napoleon pauses, remembering those days of colour and valour that will never return.

'My friend,' says Napoleon. 'My defeats, just as much as my victories, gave France a certain idea of herself. Of pride, possibilities; sadnesses and reversals, yes, but also courage, colour and glory. I didn't die old and rich in a comfortable bed. I gave France a life force. More than that, a code for living.'

Napoleon shifts his sword to a more comfortable position and smiles at Tomas.

Tereza has hung in the background and is reluctant to intrude. But there's a practical point to consider, their broken craft. 'Sir,' she asks, 'may we beg a favour?'

'Of course, mademoiselle.'

'Our craft's broken and . . . ' Napoleon holds up an arm to command silence, then brings both hands together with a resounding crash. He smiles at Tereza. It's clear the machine can travel once more in time and space.

'My friends,' Napoleon says. 'You must excuse me. Dawn is breaking and we must say farewell. Until we meet again.' With that, the Emperor and his phantom army fade into the shadows.

Kitchen etiquette . . .

The Alien's excited. Pierre is taking him to a dinner party, his first social contact with these strange creatures who raise emperors from the dead. Pierre has befriended the Alien at the new Messiah's behest and is using his investigative powers to discover some remarkable facts about a planet and species a million galaxies away.

The Alien wasn't out for a walk when he collided with the time machine, as Tereza suggested, but standing on a mountain top. This was where his telekinetic powers were strongest, in a landscape uninterrupted by the civilising works of the Alien tentacle. The Alien's society is entirely based on the telekinetic rotation of any round or spherical object. The species – sixty billion strong – even evolved physically to serve this purpose.

Just as humans breathe, Aliens rotate. But this action,

perfected over the millennia, is driven by more than a basic biological need. Their planet and all its activities – energy, transport, sport – is powered by telekinetic rotation. This particular Alien is one of its practiced masters. At the time of his mountain-top abduction he was rotating the gigantic circular turbines of the planet's power station. He is now eying an impressive rack of plates stacked artfully on the kitchen wall.

'It's only a kitchen supper,' says the hostess, who shows Pierre and the Alien around her gleaming white culinary operating theatre. 'We've just had it done.' It's now clear why dinner is in the kitchen. The hostess is bursting with pride at this mausoleum of imitation wood and marble. 'Ice?' she asks the Alien, holding up a drink. The Alien senses she wants him to say yes, so he obliges. She presses the glass against a lever in a gesture that says, 'Look, automatic dispenser.'

The Alien looks forward to some serious conversation. Perhaps he can interest everyone in the Emperor's discourse on greatness and failure. How often do people have a first-hand account of the words of France's favourite son? But he's disappointed: the only subjects of conversation are property prices and sex. As the evening goes on, and more bottles are opened, sex is discussed with ever greater urgency and animation. Perhaps his eyes are having difficulty adjusting to the earth's atmosphere – the Alien is convinced that he is seeing glimpses of swinging things and long-legged birds in the persons of his fellow diners.

Halfway through the evening, the host's children come

to say goodnight. The Alien is shocked. Humans, he's noted with pleasure, have round heads. Theirs are square, like a computer screen.

On his planet, children always eat dinner with their parents. 'We've been talking,' the children say and the Alien understands that on earth custom requires children to converse separately.

'Henry found a yellow pencil in the street today,' the girl says, 'he put it on his page and he's had hours of chat. Where did it come from? Who does it belong to? Why is it yellow?'

The Alien's confused.

'But that's not as good as Samantha,' Henry says, convulsing with laughter.

'No, Henry,' his sister interjects.

'She posted a picture of half a breast. You should see the traffic. A thousand hits.'

Their parents beam with pride and the Alien's confusion turns to bewilderment. Why do children prefer banalities to their parents' company? And why do adults allow it? Perhaps they're distracted by their new kitchen. As the evening wears on, the hostess detaches from the party to run her hand over the stainless steel hob and gaze lovingly at a pressure cooker.

'So tell me,' says Tomas when the Alien returns to the hotel, 'what discoveries did you make?'

'Children interested in nonsense, they'll grow up,' the Alien says, 'but adults and kitchens?'

'Ah yes,' replies Tomas, 'kitchen etiquette.' He pauses. 'That gives me an idea.'

TOMAS

✧

The Sermon on the Tower . . .

The earthworks are monumental, the site like that of the pyramids built two thousand years ago by slaves under the lash. Here the builders are volunteers, directed by Tomas's battalion with loud hailers. They're not building a triangle up, but digging one down.

The pit being dug at the north-east corner of the Eiffel Tower is square at its rim, but the edges taper down to the base. Half a mile wide and one hundred metres deep, the pit's slanting edges are reinforced with steel girders.

While some go down, others go up. A giant crane, the size of the tower itself, has been erected on its south-east side. The head of the crane faces the top of the tower; its steel core is as strong and thick as its neighbour's. Two arms protrude halfway up, rooting it to the ground. Thus supported, it can lift a mountain.

In between, there is an army of steel cutters. Paris reverberates to the din of electric saws slicing through the base of the Eiffel Tower, which is surprisingly light. This will make the task easier.

The River Seine runs along the north-west face of the tower. An armada of tugs is assembled there to float with the river's current. These support a huge chain, the inspiration for which came from Tomas's soup dream. The chain stretches from the tugs across the Pont d'Iéna and up the tower's north-west side. The crane holds the chain as it is lassoed to the top of the tower.

The crane detaches the lasso and hoists another teflon

chain off the ground. This is attached halfway up the tower, pulled tight like a corset. After numerous technical calculations and metallurgical tests everything is ready.

Millions of people gather behind the safety barriers to watch the commander give the order. The crane deploys, the chain becomes taut. The crowds strain to catch a glimpse of the moment of lift off. But they are disappointed. This is an inch-by-inch process and they only see the tower airborne when it is already some way off the ground, rising into the air like a giant bird from Jurassic times.

When it is fifty metres off the ground, the commander signals to the captain of the armada. A hundred engines roar as the tugs move down the river to take up the slack on the lasso. Their normal fare is battleships and ocean liners: a steel tower is no problem.

The effect of the pull down the river is as the engineers calculated. The head of the tower tilts lower as its body is raised up. A few hours later the edifice is horizontal, the top positioned over the trianglular pit. The machines are turned off and a thousand ropes manoeuvre the tower to its final resting place. It is lowered into the pit upside down, concrete pours down a chute as wide as a motorway, and soon its top is entombed in a concrete sack.

Engineers and artisans scale the sides of the inverted tower, which is two thirds of its previous height. A platform is constructed across the upturned feet. On this is laid a lawn, bisected by two pathways that form a cross. A raised podium is built at the fulcrum.

Tomas stands on it with a microphone. Giant screens

attached to the sides of the inverted tower relay his image to the tens of millions who have flocked to bear witness. From the Trocadero on the far side of the river to the Ecole Militaire in the south, even an ant would be unable to move. Moses had his mount. Now Tomas has his tower.

Banks of photographers stretch on endlessly. Reporters, beamed to their home audiences by satellite, speculate in a hundred languages as to what the first prophetic utterance of the new Messiah will be. A new set of commandments updated for modern times? Or, as the tower's inversion suggests, something more radical: a cataclysmic prophecy? Maybe he will just offer a universal message of love?

Tomas raises the microphone to his lips. Just for the hell of it, he's dressed in the flowing white robes of a priest from ancient times and is wielding Tereza's pig-beating staff for the occasion. He also sports a wispy moustache and small goatee beard, to complete the look. As he prepares to speak, his robes and hair billow in the breeze.

Two billion eyes watch Tomas calmly surveying the scene around him. He's in no hurry to begin. Only when he commands the total silence and attention of the world does he raises the microphone to his lips.

'You know a lot, I bet, about kitchen etiquette,' Tomas says.

A hundred translators whir into action; a thousand commentaries begin.

'Kitchens, like hospitals, are essential. The colours, the tiling, the trusty cooker, the fridge – maybe with an automatic ice dispenser. Then there are the accoutrements. Oh, the accoutrements! Pots and pans, ceramic mugs, giant salad bowls, the coffee machine, electric things. Tableware all matching, reassuringly expensive when bought. All symbols of your success.

'You're secure with your giant white plates, on which you serve pasta at hastily arranged dinner parties. Just sprinkle some parmesan roughly on top – that's it, that's the way. Pass the giant salad bowl; pour the red wine into the large glasses. If you lived in a voiceless world, all you'd hear would be the clink of glasses. And the tink, tink, tink of cutlery on plates at the dinner-party ballet. Clink, clink, tink, clink. Clink, clink, tink, clink, clink all evening long.

'Kitchens, you deserve your own ballet. The curtain opens on a stage of twenty kitchens, multicoloured, of differing design, the prima-donna kitchen all in white. A waltz begins. Swirl about; dance, beautiful kitchens, dance! Form a line, dance in rhythm, pass the prima-donna kitchen down the line. Now jump, dancing kitchens, leap – go on, leap! You're beautiful. Kick back your imaginary legs, unfurl your imaginary arms like flying swans who are to die in the final tragic scene.

'How tragic it would be if you came home to find that shockingly, inexplicably, a vicious sledgehammer had done its work on your kitchen. Imagine your kitchen now. The fridge stoved in with a mighty gash, the cooker irretrievably disfigured, the comfortable table splintered and everything smashed. A thousand pieces of glass and crockery, the salad bowl giant no longer. Pots and pans twisted like deformed limbs. Most horrifying of all is the shit of your assailant amid the rubbish and the rubble. And nothing else in the house disturbed, just your kitchen mangled.'

ILLUSTRATION ON
THIS PAGE

6

CANNES

ILLUSTRATION ON
THIS PAGE

7

ILLUSTRATION ON
THIS PAGE

The shining city in the sun . . .

Tomasmania sweeps the world. Sweatshops turn into ovens, all producing Tomas T-shirts. Any hotel room within a hundred miles of Paris costs a week's wages. Campsites mushroom around the city. A craze for all things French ignites. In Beijing, people bicycle home with baguettes in their baskets. Snails become as expensive as caviar. Everywhere, men take mistresses. Buildings worldwide are inverted in tribute. The Sydney Opera House looks much the same upside down, as does the Bird's Nest Stadium. In London the Eye is ingeniously inverted in one rotation.

What of the sociological reaction? Anthropologists everywhere await the start of the season with measuring tapes and binoculars. Sure enough, collars have reduced in size; breasts are no longer trolleyed but carried neatly in baskets. Hiding in a bush, a researcher hears a waiter offering to bring fresh butter. 'Please don't worry about that,' comes the reply. Hallelujah! 'Producers' struggle to practise their magic art, for street corners everywhere are now covered with warnings: 'A producer only wants one thing'; 'Come on girls, don't believe it'; and the particularly successful 'Men lie.' In a club, Tomas notices a man turning red, biting his knuckles in his efforts not to talk about money. He overhears another cancel a giant champagne bottle.

TOMAS

Tomas and Tereza have one of those magical nights: they drink just enough, dance for hours, make love and go to bed hungry and tired as dawn is breaking.

The second Messiah now needs somewhere to live, a calm, happy place whence he can propagate his message. Paris is gridlocked with followers and too grey. He wants the sun. Tomas decides to look south.

Just as the master jeweller creates the perfect mount for his stone, God created the perfect setting for Cannes. Of all the coastal resorts, Cannes is the finest. St Tropez to the west, the epicentre of trolleys and sun loungers, has its attractions, but like the rap singer's ring, it's too much. Monte Carlo to the east, home to eternal treasure keepers, is quaint but old-fashioned and as over-elaborate as a Victorian brooch. Nice in the middle has a fine historic centre but its long coastline is too much like the Queen's crown: beautiful to behold – but would you want to wear it?

Cannes is the perfect size and shape, nestling at the foot of some hills in the arc of a bay. Facing south, the seaview is framed by small mountains on the far side of the shore that snakes around the coast. Sunsets are spectacular. The seafront is less than a mile long: a dozen restaurants compete for custom and in rudeness along the beach. Behind this is the famous Croisette, a promenade lined with palm trees along which Cannois and visitors perambulate eternally.

Overlooking the Croisette are Cannes's fabulous turn-of-the-century hotels, seaside monsters like the one levitated by Tomas, all with ornate facades, balconies you can stand on and watering holes where the animals gather at six. Between them, small side streets filled with purveyors of lingerie and bikinis lead back to Cannes's main shopping street, the Rue d'Antibes, a retail paradise for every taste and budget. At the western end is the Fountainville open-air market, the best in the south, where you can eat like a king for ten euros.

With such a cornucopia of wonders, not to mention the wonderful climate, it's no surprise that Cannes is Europe's most popular festival destination. From advertising to yachts, music to mobile phones, the city is continually being flooded with festival goers plying their trade. The most famous event is, of course, the annual gathering of beautiful people for the film festival. During this period of starlets and socialites, the city morphs into a single entity, as breasts, sun loungers, champagne bottles and oversized collars blend together to create a very particular soup.

The only disappointing aspect of the city is the Palais de Festival itself. This ugly concrete structure, host to one event after another, juts out into the bay at the western end of the city. While it is functional, it appears a sorry afterthought, given the magnificence of its surroundings. It's as if the burghers of the city had sat down one day and said, 'We've got a great place here, let's turn it into a festival paradise. No need to bother with the convention hall. People will come anyway.' While Tomas understands the pragmatism of French municipal politics, the Palais de Festival is not acceptable for the second Messiah's court. He decides he needs something new.

In designing this, Tomas has an unfair advantage.

He has seen the future, and it's croissant-, beret- and garlic-shaped. The Freudian lobby argues for a baguette, another symbol of France, rampant. But in the end common sense and good taste prevail and the corporation of Cannes acquires another asset, a fabulous floating Onion.

This monument to light and space is built on a huge barge in the middle of the bay, accessed by a floating boulevard running off the Croisette. Fine green lines, imitating an onion's skin, rib the opaque white exterior, supporting the superstructure decoratively. Like the as-yet-unbuilt properties in Tomas and Tereza's time travels, the Onion is flooded with light through giant sea-facing windows. These also provide spectacular views to its occupants. But the building is practical as well as magnificent: the twisting peak of the Onion's dome houses the finest restaurant on the coast. Just as its chef garnishes a delicate dish with lemon zest, the Alien completes the Onion with a little touch of his own. Using minimal telekinetic power he sets the Onion in a permanent state of rotation at snail's pace.

Despite these wonders, the new Messiah is required to have more than one residence. He divides his time between an apartment to the rear of the city, the beachside hotels and his rotating palace on the sea. For the Russians are still trying to kill him. One night they almost succeed.

CANNES

A marsupial mishap and a giant phallus . . .

Tomas is taking Tereza to his favourite restaurant in Le Suquet. This tight pedestrian passage, where two people can barely pass, snakes up a hill to the west of the city and is home to twenty restaurants.

As Tomas and Tereza ascend they are thrown against a wall by a kangaroo. The commotion behind them signifies an accident, and they watch the kangaroo disappear up the hill, its leash trailing in the air.

The prelude to this mishap began several days ago when Boss Olgarv rented a room above one of the restaurants. The problem of transporting a four-hundred-pound kangaroo up the narrow staircase to its new home was solved by means of a powerful Russian sedative. Even stronger Russian hands manhandled the sleeping giant up the stairs.

On waking, the marsupial wasn't happy. Given miles of Australian outback or a cramped room in Cannes in which to jump, the choice was obvious. But the kangaroo was part of a plan which required only one, possibly his final, jump. His loud and malodorous protests were covered by the equally strong exudations from the passageway below. Anyway this is the Mediterranean. Live and let live.

Boss Olgarv's plan was absurdly simple. On the appointed night, he would wait for the diners to throng the narrow street. Then, having brought the kangaroo to the window, he would push the unfortunate animal off the ledge. Its target, Tomas's head, would, according to Boss Olgarv's calculations and the laws of physics, be crushed like an almond in a nutcracker. The plan also paid tribute to the many assassinations perpetrated by the motherland, in which journalists and other undesirables are despatched using farcical methods that render both the cause of death and the assassin's identity instantly obvious to the world.

Despite the brilliance of the idea it doesn't work. At the critical moment, the sharp-sighted Alien, now acting as the new Messiah's twirling praetorian, notices a large spherical shape – Boss Olgarv's stomach – overhead. Taking no chances, he rotates it immediately. This spooks the marsupial, who changes its appointed trajectory and lands on another spot with powerful legs. Boss Olgarv is caught off guard. His hand, attached to the leash, follows the beast earthwards, as do his arm and body. He lands on his head and is killed instantly, while the kangaroo, after days of dreaming about open spaces, jumps off to find some.

The autopsy, presided over by Judge Reynard, is an unpleasant affair. His detachable stomach, which exploded on impact, is a bloody mess of flesh and gore. But in amongst the guts and blubber the physicians discover a secret compartment, the contents of which are brought immediately to the judge's attention.

The judge spreads a bloodied drawing before Tomas. It's the most bizarre thing they have ever seen. It appears to be of a phallus with gigantic testicles. As they scrape away the muck and grime, the picture becomes clear.

The drawing marked 'Cocksack' – presumably in homage to Cossack – is of a soldier in a phallus-shaped uniform with his face exposed through a hole cut at the top and his arms through side openings. The phallus doesn't have feet; its means of locomotion, the judge deduces, must be jumping. The phallus soldier wears a Cossack sword and carries what appears to be a detonator in one hand. But the uniform's most distinctive feature is the pair of enormous testicles that is attached to the front. These are of the same size and design as Boss Olgarv's stomach.

'Boss Olgarv has created a uniform in his own image,' says the judge. 'But what function could such giant appendages possibly perform?'

Tomas looks at another drawing that shows a cut-away section. 'The testicles appear to be huge containers of some sort,' he says. 'Look, there's a tube running up the soldier's back to the top of his head and a pumping mechanism. And the whole thing's connected to a detonator.' He turns grey. He has just survived a third assassination attempt. Now this, a Cocksack soldier, probably a prototype for millions, featuring a device to spread all manner of evil.

Reynard, too, understands the implications. 'Tomas,' he says. 'You've achieved a lot. But sermons won't work against this enemy. We must consider something more drastic.'

'Very well,' says Tomas. 'I'll raise the Emperor.'

The fable of the fence . . .

Tomas finds the great man in a beautiful wooded glade by the sea, a few kilometres from Cannes. Two hundred years ago, Napoleon landed here with a handful of followers to reclaim his crown. Sunlight filters through the trees, illuminating the Emperor and making dappled patterns on the ground.

TOMAS

Napoleon is leaning against a small section of fence in the middle of a group of people to whom he appears to be giving orders. But these aren't followers, they're students. And the Emperor's not giving orders, he's teaching. Napoleon looks up as Tomas enters the glade.

'Forgive my intrusion, Sir,' Tomas says, embarrassed. 'I've come to seek your counsel.'

'Think nothing of it,' Napoleon replies. 'Please, join us.'

A space is made for Tomas and he sits cross-legged on the ground like a school child. He looks confused.

'What do you think we do in the hereafter?' asks Napoleon. 'Sleep?' He sweeps his arms in a wide gesture. Tomas glances around the glade. 'No, each develops his skill; there are artisans, cooks, athletes, even poets. Thankfully, there's not much need for generalship, so I teach.'

'May I enquire which subject?' Tomas asks. Napoleon looks at his pupils, amused.

'There's only one subject,' he replies. 'Once you've mastered it, there's no further need for teachers. You can then learn anything you wish by yourself.'

Tomas's gazes at him helplessly.

'Come, Tomas. Guess.'

He continues to stare blankly, quite at a loss. 'Philosophy?' he mumbles weakly.

'Very well,' says Napoleon. 'Let me help you. In the temporal world there are thousands of educational symbols and mottos. Shields with Latin words I find difficult to understand. Mortar boards and academic gowns, the purpose of which is unclear to me. Fine sayings: "Receive the light that you may give it forth"; "Not only intelligence, but also virtue"; "Wisdom and knowledge shall be the stability of thy times."

'Here, there is only one educational symbol – the fence. This doesn't manifest itself as a logo or motto but as a physical presence, which students see each day.'

'And what does the fence represent?' Tomas asks.

'The worst possible thing in life – or death,' Napoleon replies. 'Mediocrity; those who strive for nothing. Fence-sitters who think of nothing beyond their base needs – sex, money, alcohol. People who won't defend a friend or principle at all costs, who are the first to drift away in a fight. People who are stuck, who settle for second best and are incapable of mental mobility – of enquiry, discovery or wonder – whose domain is the sofa and, worse still, the fence.'

'So being sent to sit on the fence is like standing in the corner?'

'That is not its purpose. The corner is a form of punishment. The fence is a symbol of mediocrity, which students in the afterlife are taught to repudiate. It's enough that it's there.'

'But not all people are able,' Tomas argues; 'most live ordinary lives.'

'Ability and role in life have nothing to do with it. You can be an exceptional street cleaner but a mediocre political leader,' Napoleon replies.

'How can a mediocrity lead a nation?'

'Very easily. Let's say that the leader, when elected, inherits a strong stable country. The time calls for small incremental improvements to the nation's wellbeing. It's not glamorous, but he needs to focus on the details in areas like health, education, law and order and ensure prudence and safety in the nation's finances. But he's a glory seeker. He talks about his legacy, and wishes to feel the hand of history on his shoulder. He doesn't understand that it's fortune's wheel, not the individual, which determines greatness; that glory isn't given to every leader. If the times call for a great deed, so be it. If not, it's a disaster to seek it out.

'So instead of concentrating on the basics, he becomes entangled in foreign adventures in the name of making the world a better place. When they go wrong, he speaks with the serpent tongue of a lawyer justifying what he's done. But excuses aren't good enough – it's his job not to make mistakes. And since these were caused by his glory-seeking in the first place, it's so much the worse. Instead of the epitaph "Here lies a great man", he's given "Here lies a mediocrity".'

'I understand,' says Tomas, 'how the glory seeker is mediocre. But what about ordinary people? How do you free yourself once stuck on the fence?'

' "Stuck" is a short way of saying "mediocre",' Napoleon replies. 'The answer is self-realisation. Look at your situation. Are you trapped in a job, relationship, home or way of thinking? Do you confuse trivia with what is important? Are you bad tempered about small things? "Disaster! My dinner's late." Do you feel the light fading and your waist expanding? If the answer is "Yes", then you need to take some risks and be prepared to fail.'

'That's easier said than done.'

'Is it? Can't you send out a hundred CVs; try harder or finish with your girlfriend; buy a one-way ticket out of town; retrain; go to night school; emigrate; think, discover, internet your way to a different life? Isn't effort rewarded, and trying always worth it? Anything but the twilight world of bitterness, prejudice, alcohol and bad language.'

'And if you're a lifelong mediocrity?' asks Tomas.

'Priests will tell you,' Napoleon replies, 'that sins can be forgiven and wrongs righted. You might be glued to the fence for a lifetime. But one day, just before the end, decide not to be just another echo on the wind.'

That night, Tomas dreams that he's in an arena, surrounded by a cheering crowd. Trumpets sound, the Emperor arrives and the games begin. Huge iron gates swing open and a hundred collar wearers riding mobile fences charge at him. In their haste, their collars get caught in the fence sections; they trip and fall in a heap. Next, an army of trolley wheelers wielding fence posts attempts to run him down. The trolleys are made for style, not speed – their wheels detach and Tomas bounces against soft flesh. Finally, a thousand leviathan champagne bottles lined up on top of a fence fire their corks simultaneously. Tomas uses his magic trick of slowing time and the corks stop in the air and fall to the ground. He wins the first round.

Trumpets sound again. Out of nowhere, a Russian yacht with a nasty rotating propeller materialises and advances on Tomas. This looks like trouble. Then an even bigger oligarch boat appears to join the attack. Double trouble. What's this? A still larger Soviet battleship, that has been converted into a floating palace with savage motor blades, is bearing down on him as well. Tomas is just about to be shredded when the cry goes up, 'Yours is bigger than mine,' and again, 'Yours is bigger than mine.' The boats forget about Tomas and start chasing each other around the arena with ever increasing velocity. The result is a delicious yacht soup, which the crowd drinks. Tomas wins again.

Napoleon summons Tomas. 'To the victor the spoils,' he says. 'Ask any question you wish.'

'What is needed to defeat the Cocksack army?'

'Power,' the Emperor replies.

Tomas wakes up and shakes Tereza from her sleep. 'Being the new Messiah isn't enough. The presidential election's soon. You're going to stand.'

'And how do you propose I become President of the Republic?'

'With the help of my enemies.'

The ultimate aphrodisiac . . .

There are many types of aphrodisiac, from foods and potions to candlelit dinners by the sea. Some people think of oysters when the word is mentioned, others of mind-changing substances. It is generally agreed, however, that the most succulent fruits on the aphrodisiac tree are power and money. Of these, power is the more delicious.

Presidents of the Republic have made liberal and un-subtle use of this potent balm since time began. The current incumbent, a believer in tradition, is no exception. He's so confident about the supernatural effect of his four magic words that he throws caution to the wind whenever he uses them.

'I am the President,' he says, as one might say: 'It's a nice day'; 'You're a woman'; or, 'There's a nose on my face.' Whereas these statements might be answered with a simple, 'Yes, I agree,' the 'I am the President' aphrodisiac, put through the translator, takes on a different meaning. It always elicits the desired response. Thus . . .

STATEMENT: I am the President.
TRANSLATION: Fuck me immediately.

The four uncompromising words, reduced to three in translation, compel the hearer to undress immediately and prepare for coupling. While this satisfies the President, it's rather less obvious what benefits accrue to the recipients of his largesse. It's one of the great unanswered questions of history. The girl fucks instantly and without ceremony. Then what? A mention in the credits?

As the new Messiah's girlfriend, it's not difficult for Tereza to arrange a meeting with the President. Now, she stands before him in the private salon of the presidential residence not far from Cannes.

'To what do I owe this pleasure, madamoiselle?' the President asks.

Tereza looks coy. She twists one leg suggestively but keeps her eyes fixed on the President.

'Madamoiselle, may I help you?' he says.

Tereza bites her lip lightly.

TOMAS

The President rises from his desk of state – where Napoleon once sat – and walks towards Tereza.

She wears a simple brown dress, with matching high heels. Her only jewellery is a chunky pendant the size of a small camera lens. Her smooth legs shimmer with a hint of oil. As he approaches, the President catches a glimpse of her perfect upturned breasts. Just as he reaches her, she lowers her eyes, sways shyly and twists a strand of hair.

This is it. One, two, three.

'Madamoiselle, I am the President,' he says.

Nothing. Tereza remains impassive.

'I repeat. I am the President.'

Tereza turns a foot inwards.

'Do I make myself plain, mademoiselle?' the President asks, his passion rising.

'Forgive me, Monsieur le President,' Tereza says. 'I'm so sorry. I don't understand what that means.' Thrusting out her chest, she raises her eyes to meet his and opens her mouth.

The President explodes with frustration and desire. 'Fuck me immediately!' he shrieks. 'Immediately, I say. Fuck me immediately.'

'Very well,' says Tereza and turns on her heel and leaves the room.

Moments later, their meeting is broadcast worldwide on Shit TV.

In the battle between sex and something else . . .

. . . something else always loses. The presidential election is one such battle.

Tereza's broadcast meeting with the President is a ratings triumph on a par with her Hank-torture series. She becomes Shit TV's new star. And why not? She is young, sexy and the girlfriend of the new Messiah, with endless potential for mischief. What else does a star need? Or a President for that matter?

In unleashing its campaign, Shit TV finds that the President is an easy target: the French don't object so much to the use of the presidential aphrodisiac as to its failure. It shames the *Patrie* for the President to command 'open sesame' only for the magic portal to remain shut.

He doesn't go down without a fight. He closets himself with his advisers. They go days without sleep. The presidential nails are bitten to the quick. As much French blood, sweat and tears are shed as on a Napoleonic battlefield. At last, one early dawn – eureka! The President hits on a winning idea, a political ideology of such brilliance and originality that all will be swept before it.

Change! A concept so unfamiliar in contemporary politics that – who knows? – he may even be hailed as the second Napoleon.

He had been planning a campaign based on truth: 'Citizens! I regret there's not much we can do with our great nation. We're stuck. Whatever is promised, nothing ever happens. It's all just talk and air. Let's not worry. Water has a way of finding its own level. Time will resolve what we politicians are unable to do. I, at least, am straight about the situation. So vote for me.'

The new version: 'Citizens! You're not stupid – you would never fall for an idea that's been used a thousand times before. Especially not a political cliché that is as old as the hills and is known never to work. So here's a brilliant new one – change! Never promised before by any politician, and guaranteed to work. So vote for me.'

Although the President doesn't realise it, the world is, in fact, the subject of a cosmic joke perpetrated by God. One day, for no particular reason, he waved his hand and fixed the world in a perpetual time warp, the effect of which was that nothing has ever changed in politics. It is almost as if the world gets into a giant time machine, ready for an exciting political journey, only to hear a crunching of gears and a loud bang. Instead of travelling among the stars, we are stuck for eternity. Luckily, the people are unaware of this celestial prank and exult in the President's brilliant new idea.

Election day arrives and Tereza and Shit TV have a problem. What can compete with the President's superb political marketing of rupture, the need for change, a break with the past, a fresh beginning, the nation reborn, the dawning of a new day?

'There's nothing for it,' says Tereza.

She strips live on Shit TV. And wins by a landslide.

Rats and respect . . .

A rat can fit through a space the size of a pencil. Millions of rodents now perform this trick to invade every place of incarceration in the world that houses violent criminals: murderers, armed robbers, weapon-toting narcotics and people traffickers, street thugs and mafiosi.

The rats squeeze and scurry through holes and up drainpipes carrying tiny pieces of equipment, which they deposit in every prison canteen before scuttling off for more. Groups of technicians assemble the equipment with twitching whiskers and busy paws. The process is arduous and assembly slow but the rat sea swarms and surges and each tide brings a little more progress. Gradually the equipment begins to take shape.

The precursor to this global infestation was the Great Bear's angry summons to King Rat. Tereza's election is inconsequential; she and the fake Messiah will be swept aside in the coming deluge but for Shit TV to endorse her in its desperation for ratings is an abomination. The Great Bear knows that the fake Messiah despises Shit TV; the network was responsible for his death and his very existence is an antidote to everything it stands for. Doesn't the network know it's being played for a fool? That by conniving with him, it sows the seeds of its own destruction?

This is King Rat's mission: to return Shit TV to the Great Bear's cause; to promote licentiousness, the worship of money, depravity of every hue and colour – all to soften the West for the final broadcast. His master has prepared a thousand times in his mind. That of his new world empire. For the army is half mobilised, its weapons almost ready and with the Cocksacks disgorged of their venomous load and Tomas's broken body at his feet, the Great Bear will finally emerge from his lair. Only the biggest network in world history will suffice as a platform from which to proclaim the new Russian hegemony.

For King Rat, it's an easy mission. Shit TV's only interest is programming. He just needs to think up a suitably profane show in order to be guaranteed a platform for his master's message come the great day.

In perfecting his plan, he plays on the one characteristic that is shared by all men of violence – stupidity. How fortunate for him that the global justice system, so obsessed with reason and fairness, has failed to exploit this flaw. It would have saved a lot of trouble. King Rat is about to conduct a masterclass in annihilation without even breaking the law.

As prison canteens around the world fill for the morning meal, convicts are greeted by a giant screen set up against a wall, with a projection device attached to the ceiling overhead. Cameras and other broadcasting para-phernalia are positioned around the eating areas. The criminals collect breakfast, scratch their heads and sit down to watch.

The screens flicker into life and King Rat appears. 'Today I want to talk about respect,' he says. This is a word they understand. They lean forward to listen. 'What's the difference between you and other men? Why do they scuttle like ants while you walk like lions? The answer's simple. Respect. You have it – they don't. They know nothing of the street. Of real life. Of what it takes to be a man.

'Each of you wears a badge of honour. Prison. Doing your time. The elementary mark of respect. Without it no other honours are possible. It is an absolute necessity.

'There are grades to this order, aren't there? Your second, third, fourth, fifth sentences. As you reoffend and return to gaol, fellow inmates nod in deference and make gestures of solidarity and obeisance to the really hard man. You can take it. Even more respect.

'Most of you here have earned the second badge of honour – violence. The rite of passage: to cut and be cut. That's your motto. Smash his arm; break his leg; splinter his nose. You're men of blood. Other people – get the fuck out of the way. Respect.

'A few of you wear the third badge – murder. The final mark of manhood. Shoot your enemy in the face. Stab him through the heart. Respect.

'If a man snatches a glance at your woman, knife him in the eye. If he dares a second glimpse? Kill the bastard. Disrespect. He deserves it. Then do your orang-utan walk, roll your hips; slouch, sway, swagger down the street. Do your special clicks and flicks. Curl your lip in a menacing snarl. You're in the jungle now, an animal. That's it. That's the way. Perfect. Respect.

'But as I look about me now I see no one bearing the badge of the highest order: the ultimate accolade in respect's pantheon of greatness. How could I? You're all alive.

'Think about it. Who do you honour most? Who is

spoken of with the greatest reverence and awe? Whose lives and deeds are told and retold without end? The answer is the dead. The narco slaughtered in a hail of bullets. The Mafia boss killed from behind with a knife. The gang member murdered with a machete. Theirs is the true greatness that comes only with death. The ultimate respect.

'What is prison, violence and murder compared to dying a real man's death? Aren't all heroes remembered thus? Why are you still alive? What are you waiting for? Do you have girls' parts beneath those breeches?

'Get up! Earn the highest badge of honour. It makes perfect sense. Kill and be killed. Take up your chairs. Smash each other's heads! Jab a spoon into the next man's eye! Throttle him! Pulp his face!

'Do this so that this day will be remembered, and your names with it. The day when the hardest men in history came together with one voice, and in one moment joined in a final fraternal embrace, together glorying in the highest order of respect – death.'

Educational time travels . . .

Tomas and Tereza are amazed. A group of Taiwanese schoolgirls in pretty red uniforms are smiling, laughing and waving at them – two thousand feet up in the air. They're in the time machine gliding over the South China Sea in the year 3000, and are joined in flight by an altogether bigger craft – the island of Taiwan!

This odyssey follows the mutual annihilation of two

million violent criminals live on Shit TV, the biggest ratings triumph of all time – with the promise at the end of the show of an even bigger surprise next week. This is it. The Great Bear's final plan.

Tomas visits the Emperor urgently to give him a situation report. The Cocksacks are massing on the Polish border; their testicles carry a secret weapon he assumes to be lethal; the West has been weakened by Shit TV and people are so venal and stupid that they might even support the invasion in the belief that it is connected to next week's programme; power has been gained via Tereza's presidency but this alone can't withstand the Russian attack. The position is desperate. What must he do?

In response to his breathless plea, Napoleon delivers a history lesson.

'When I fought Russia two hundred years ago,' he says, 'my army advanced into the Great Bear's motherland. The Russians joined battle from time to time but always retreated, drawing us in deeper. The winter brought a cold so chilling that fingers froze on cannons and breath became ice in the air. Eventually my army was immobilised. Only then did the Great Bear leave his lair to annihilate us.'

'One hundred and fifty years later, in another great war, exactly the same thing happened. An army attacked Russia, it was drawn in and destroyed. You now have the power over men and machines. So you tell me, what must you do?'

Tomas and Tereza have set off in the time machine to find out how to draw the Great Bear out and trap him.

This seemingly impossible mission isn't helped by their bizarre encounter. The console provides an explanation.

A few centuries earlier, the ingenious Taiwanese invented a technology whereby the atoms of their island's submerged landmass were violently vibrated together. When particles in the atmosphere were similarly treated, a vacuum was created, the effect of which was to lift the island off the seabed. With a speed and steerage system attached, the island became mobile.

Taiwan is on its way to its annual holiday in the Caribbean. But the technology provides an unexpected bonus. On its travels, the island stops over China, where the population leans over the edge to hurl insults and rotten things at its hated neighbour.

China's loss of pride here is regained elsewhere. Travelling over another landmass, Tomas and Tereza notice a remarkable transformation – Africa has become Chinese.

While other empires messed about over the millennia, the Chinese got busy. Looking at the long term, under-developed Africa was identified as having potential, with the consequence that, over centuries, Chinese money, technology and knowhow flooded its shores. By 3000 the dark continent has become yellow. It speaks, eats and even breakbeats Chinese.

America has undergone a similar transformation. This started in the mid twenty-fifth century when Mexico, tired of playing the poor relation, hatched an ingenious plan. Over decades, a giant subterranean cavern was built in secret on the American border. Tens of millions of Mexicans were assembled. On the appointed day, a whistle blew and a thousand pontoon bridges straddled the Rio Grande. Within days, fifty million Mexicans crossed the border, aided by generations of previous immigrants. The border guards put up a fight and several thousand intruders were captured. But in the end numbers prevailed and Mexico took over. The eagle replaced the Stars and Stripes. Americans now sleep in the afternoon, have dinner at ten and love their mothers. The result? A much happier nation.

Tomas and Tereza's favourite discovery, however, is the Omnipotent Musical Being, whose appearance on the world stage is as bizarre as it's unexpected. The Being never really bothered with the world until one day his giant finger accidentally pressed one of the palazzi lining Venice's Grand Canal. The palazzo was instantly submerged into the mud of the lagoon, making a 'Parp!' noise like an organ note. Due to the Being's lightness of touch and his other omnipotent qualities, it bounced up again undamaged. Amused, the Being tried it on the palazzo's neighbour. It too submerged, made a different sounding 'Parp!' and then resurfaced. The Being ordered all the palazzi cleared. Thousands of Venetians were temporarily dehoused.

Looking at the sky above the city, you are now likely to see the fingers of two huge hands interlocked and cracking together in a limbering-up exercise. After a few preparatory 'Parps!' to establish pitch and tone, the Omnipotent Musical Being plays the palazzi in concert like the keys of a giant organ.

At first the Venetians were furious at this intrusion into their floating paradise and the damage caused by mud and silt. But the city often floods – and the music is beautiful. The Being's concerts quickly became a gigantic tourist attraction. Gondolas groan under the weight of euphoric fans. The residents, far from angry, dress in bathing suits and snorkels, and ride their palazzi up and down like vertical aquatic rollercoasters.

Predictably, the world has become a Federation by the year 3000 and fought several successful interstellar wars. Buoyed by these victories, the Federation challenges another star system, only to be defeated in seconds by an opponent who covers the sun with a giant black dot.

On their way home Tomas and Tereza see a beautiful sphere floating in space. Like the pockets of a roulette wheel, bright diamond sections alternate with luminescent black elements around its circumference. Bemused, Tomas asks the invisible voice for his opinion.

'Come on,' says the invisible voice, 'take a guess. A sphere rotating in time and space with alternate light and dark sections. It can only be one thing.' Tomas and Tereza scratch their heads. 'It's the wheel of fortune.'

How to dig a trench . . .

'The new Messiah has gone mad,' screams Shit TV's news bulletin. 'He's attempting to amputate Italy's foot.'

While Tomas's sanity may be in question, the accuracy of Shit TV's report isn't. The boot-shaped peninsula runs over seven hundred miles from Milan down to Naples, with a clearly defined foot at the lower end. Tomas has drawn a line at the top of the foot, from Camerota on the west coast to Bari on the east, a distance of around one hundred miles. He orders a mile-deep trench to be dug from coast to coast.

In this he is aided, as ever, by the Alien, who uses his telekinetic magic to transport a fleet of digging machines with rotating circular drills to the trench site. In flight, with parts in motion, they resemble a swarm of prehistoric creatures migrating south. These mechanical mammoths now go to work on the trench. The serrated edges of their drills resemble jagged teeth; viewed from space, it appears that a rogue army of mutant machines is chewing off Italy's foot.

The monster excavators are operated by the combined armies of the West. This gigantic mobilisation was suggested by the new President, who used the potent combination of her charms and her authority to persuade her aging male counterparts to fall in with the plan.

Meanwhile a unit of engineers has been positioned at Bari, its task to sink a massive pin into the earth at the top right-hand corner of the amputated foot. This object, many times larger than the rotating rod in Tomas's Russian-soup dream, is half a mile wide and two miles long. Massive piling machines drive it into the earth's core.

The new Messiah's plans don't just involve moving dirt, and it's not only the army that is busy. Next, Tomas orders a series of chains to be attached along the length of the south coast from Siderno to Tricase at its heel. These are driven into the coastal rock and then hoisted aboard the ships of the West's combined fleet. Once secured, the ships begin to sail south-east towards Greece.

Rat spies swarm the trench site and coastal areas. Their

reports defy belief. The military and naval strength of the West is massed around the foot of Italy. A trench is being dug, in an apparent attempt to remove it. Simultaneously, the biggest armada in world history is carrying hundreds of heavy chains, all secured to the shoreline, out to sea.

The Great Bear can't believe the scale of Tomas's miscalculation. The skill of the defending commander is to anticipate the time and place of the enemy attack. How could he possibly believe that the entire Cocksack army would invade south through Italy? Even a novice would spread his forces across the West in expectation of an advance on several fronts. And to make his main line of defence so obvious? Perhaps he really is insane; will he go from the sermon on the tower, to a soliloquy in a trench?

The West is wide open. The Great Bear orders the strike.

'Cocks away!'

Despite the screeching sirens that warn of invasion, Pierre, as Tomas's reporter-in-chief, still receives telephone calls and information. He has just heard from the hypnotherapist whom he recommended to the smoking soldier. Apparently the therapy didn't work, the patient's head was 'blocked'. His investigation of the new Messiah never ends. It's evening and he is sitting with Judge Reynard in a suite of a Cannes hotel attempting to question him above the noise. What else can he do? He has written more words than anyone attacking the Great Bear. Now that he has failed to discover the secret of the pipeline extension, there's just one last piece left to write – the destruction of the West. Soon, however, he'll be dead, a condition unhelpful to storytelling. He might as well go down chasing his original quarry.

This one is difficult to catch, not least because he has gone mad. 'Has Tomas ever exhibited signs of dementia to you?' Pierre asks the judge. 'Has he behaved irrationally or as if on drugs?'

'Not at all,' Reynard replies above the wail. 'He was perhaps a little soporific after his execution; otherwise I have always found him to be clear minded, normal.'

'I've always meant to ask you,' Pierre continues casually, 'why someone as organised and thoughtful as yourself neglected Tomas's funeral arrangements?'

'Did you say organised and thoughtful?' the judge replies, 'or old and forgetful? As you know, I don't have much time and . . . '

He is cut off by a tremendous crash as an anti-aircraft battery in the nearby fort fires a salvo into the night. With the regular army away in south Italy, the local militia are defending the town with equipment left over from a forgotten war. It's not just the judge who hasn't much time: the searchlight, normally used for celebrity parties and film premieres, now illuminates an approaching apocalypse.

Just as the sea is composed of water, God intended the sky to be made of clouds. On this night over Cannes, it consists of an undulating blanket of metal, which causes the first ever unscheduled eclipse of the moon. Thousands of aircraft are flying in formation overhead, the roar of their engines creating an airborne earthquake that cracks the pavements and knocks the elderly off their feet.

A worse terror awaits within their metal skins. Perched on rooftops and balconies, the Cannois hear a terrible groan of undercarriages opening; moments later they behold the instruments of the Great Bear's Armageddon: a thousand giant phalluses, with massive distended testicles dangling beneath them, are hurtling like meteors towards the city.

By daybreak every street corner in London, Paris, Berlin and Rome is occupied by a Cocksack. Ten million have fallen over Europe the previous night to take up their positions; a further army is massed in reserve on the Polish border. Now each Cocksack soldier peers with an expressionless face through the hole in his phallus's head, awaiting the order via his mobile headset, detonator ready.

A deathly pall falls over the West. Not a breeze stirs. Just as Tomas puts the finishing touch to his trench and the chains become taut, King Rat begins the countdown.

'Attention, Cocksacks! Three, two . . . '

A cream puff destroys the world . . .

On the night of the Cocksack invasion, Mrs Olgarv sends her husband a death dream. Like him, she's not very good at transmitting telepathic messages to the dead. It requires mental dexterity to stop the dream veering off in the wrong direction. But it's the thought that counts. In this instance, Mrs Olgarv believes the Boss deserves a nice dream. The West is being invaded and will collapse come dawn, and the Cocksacks, designed to his order and in his image, will carry the day. Although the Boss can't rejoice in the temporal world he can at least have some fun in the great hereafter.

Boss Olgarv dreams that he's having lunch at a seaside restaurant in Cannes on the day after the invasion. The restaurant has been cleared of all other diners, tables and chairs, and a simple reinforced slab is set in the middle, on to which the Boss climbs. He is wearing his detachable stomach and, in deference to the events of the previous day, a pair of gigantic testicles.

The Boss lies down on the slab. A pillow is placed beneath his head and he is made comfortable by the waiters. He opens his mouth, whereupon two large tubes are fed down his throat. The Boss signals his readiness and service begins.

Anticipating his arrival, the restaurant staff have raided all the nearby kitchens. The produce acquired – meat, fish, vegetables, fruit, pastries, pasta, bread, cheese, eggs – is piled into a giant liquidiser and pulped into a fetid grey mess. This is now pumped into Boss Olgarv via the first connecting tube, as a main course. The Boss is told that a gargantuan cream puff awaits him for dessert. It's the size of a swimming pool: he looks forward to diving in.

Filling the second gastric pipeline involved a separate assault on all the cellars in Cannes. A river of vodka is poured through a funnel down the second tube.

Boss Olgarv greatly enjoys his celebratory meal. The waiters gather round to perform small services. An escaping food particle is dabbed from his mouth; his brow is caressed with a chilled cloth; his stomach is massaged to ease its labours.

ILLUSTRATION ON
THIS PAGE

8

ILLUSTRATION ON
THIS PAGE

Eventually the Boss signals that he is satiated and the tubes are removed. A dozen waiters attempt to prop him up on the slab but he's so full and fat that it is impossible. Worse, their efforts disturb the finely balanced eco-system of the Boss's stomach and he is violently sick.

The waiters rush to fetch buckets and mops to clean up the mess, while the maître d' politely suggests that the Boss might want to rest awhile after his exertions. 'What?' screams Boss Olgarv. 'You think I can't handle the cream puff? This is an insult to Russia.' Although the French Riviera has been subjugated, the maître d' deserves worse, the Boss rants. Slavery is too good for him. He must be killed. In fact, why stop there? Destroy the restaurant. Why not Cannes? France deserves it as well. Hell, blow up the world! Boss Olgarv orders nuclear Armaggedon.

Russia has the power to destroy the world a hundred times over. Once or twice isn't enough. Not an ant shall remain. This is exactly what happens. To Boss Olgarv's satisfaction, the world is destroyed not once, but a hundred times over.

The giant cream puff, the cause of the catastrophe, is also obliterated, except for a blob of whipped cream which somehow manages to escape the nuclear hell fires. This is dragged by an ant to its lair beneath the restaurant. The cream blob sustains the ant during the winter of the nuclear holocaust, precipitating an entirely unexpected result.

A radiation particle permeates the ant's nest and bonds with the blob. When ingested it has an immediate and dramatic effect. The ant mutates.

Despite the devastation of the world, there's still more

damage to be done. The restaurant's mosaic floor is split asunder as a giant mutated ant emerges into the dawn of the post-nuclear day. It has grown not just in size, but in intelligence too.

It takes the ant only hours to find the materials – mostly from people's kitchens – necessary to construct a time machine, and a few more to complete the task. He mutates a million of his fellow soldiers, who in turn build a million machines. They return in time to Russia just before Boss Olgarv orders the strike and switch off all the computers. Russia is thus enslaved for eternity by an army of mutated time-travelling ants.

'Idiot!' screams the Great Bear at Boss Olgarv.

'Damn,' he replies. 'Next time I'll eat the cream puff before ordering the strike. That'll get the ant.'

Judge Reynard and the dream devil . . .

As the Cocksacks tumble to earth, Judge Reynard is philosophical about what the morning will bring. He's ill and will die soon anyway. A little less time, so what? Nevertheless, he is unable to spend a peaceful last night because in his dream he is presiding over the trial of the Devil.

'You are accused of unspeakable evil,' a prosecutor opens, 'of perpetrating untold crimes of misery, mayhem and murder, of destroying civilisations and corrupting souls, and leading billions into temptation; of spreading pestilential disease and death. How do you plead?'

'Not guilty,' replies a defence lawyer.

A barrage of defence arguments ensue.

'My client is not of this world; therefore he is not subject to its laws,' says one.

'Without evil, how can we understand good?' says another. 'My client in fact does mankind a service and should be rewarded.'

'Define good and evil,' says a third. 'What were the Christian crusaders, or the conquistadors who exterminated the Aztecs, good or evil?'

'This is madness,' says Judge Reynard. 'Your client is obviously guilty. He's the Devil. No further debate is necessary. Does he have anything to say before I pass sentence?'

The Devil burnishes his horns with a cleft hand. His forked tail flicks in the air behind him. His yellow eyes focus on the judge. Clearly he's thinking hard. Eventually he stands, leans forward and, stroking his beard with long hoary fingers, makes the judge a proposition.

'If I tell you how to rid the world of evil,' says the Devil, 'will you spare me death?'

'A fine fantasy,' says a prosecuting lawyer.

'Your Honour?' asks the Devil.

Judge Reynard considers the proposition. On the one hand, he should be sentenced summarily. He is, after all, the Devil. On the other, this is an unusual case, plea bargains are part of the legal system and besides, he's curious.

'Proceed,' says the judge.

'Imagine a world,' the Devil says, 'where you can walk anywhere at night, leave your house unlocked and keys in the car. Where drugs and street deals don't exist and trafficking is a thing of the past. Imagine never hearing reports of an old lady being attacked or reading of the horrific work of a repeat offender. Graffiti becomes an art form. Mankind without ghettos, cartels, mafioso, gangs. In short, a world free of crime.'

'Inconceivable,' a prosecutor says.

'Is it?' the Devil replies. 'What if by imprisoning two million of seven billion people it became a reality?'

The court stirs. This smacks of summary justice. And the legal profession is liberal by nature. In any event, it isn't possible and a prosecuting lawyer says so.

'Are you certain?' the Devil replies. 'The tiniest fraction of people organise crime. I should know, I create them. Street gangs, mafia cartels; narcotics and people-trafficking groups; families of hoodlums and miscreants. The police know exactly who they are. They could be arrested in a week.'

'This is the language of the Middle Ages,' a prosecutor says from the bench. 'Are you suggesting that we return to the law of the jungle? Even a beast has rights.' He sits down to a murmur of approval.

'You were once asked,' the Devil addresses Judge Reynard, 'whether a small means justifies a greater end? Would you summarily execute a future dictator in the knowledge it would save millions of lives?'

'The answer is obvious,' the judge replies, 'one life in exchange for millions.'

'So what's the difference?' the Devil says. 'Under my dominion, a few people subject millions to every imaginable abuse, degradation, addiction and perversion. Whole countries and communities are immobilised by fear, not to mention the economic cost. Is it such a price?'

'There may be a different perspective,' says one of the Devil's defence lawyers. 'I was a soldier before I became a lawyer. My business was battle but I see no difference between crime and war. If anything, crime's worse. It's more pernicious, surreptitiously evil like my client, death by a thousand cuts. As least in war there's sometimes a principle involved. Crime is only ever about money. We're often promised clampdowns on crime. But they never work. Why not treat it as war?'

'Very well,' says Judge Reynard, 'we incarcerate all known criminals in the world. Then what?'

'Abolish juries and have a two-strike system,' says the Devil.

The court erupts. Abolish juries? That is almost dictatorship. And why only two strikes? The soldier lawyer steps in to invite the Devil to explain.

'You need to turn what is slow and complicated,' the Devil says, 'into something fast and simple. No more juries who neither care nor want to be there, sitting like hens doing their knitting. Instead, panels of judges who've seen it all before. Trials would take days, instead of weeks, months or years. Justice would be swift and expert.'

'And the two strikes?' asks the soldier lawyer.

'That makes things simple for the criminal. First strike: understanding, forgiveness; no time, cost or effort spared in the attempt to rehabilitate. That should please your God. Second strike – it's over. The murderer seeking a weapon within hours of release. The rapist stalking his victim on his first day of freedom. No more appeals, paroles, loopholes, remissions, reductions or sentences that say one thing but mean another.'

'And how is this to be achieved?' asks Judge Reynard.

'Stop listening to lawyers who are paid by the hour. Do you think they want speed? As for simplicity, how does that serve their puffed-up speeches? And what of the lawyers directly under my influence? The attorney of a Mafia boss; does he believe his client is innocent? Or the defender of an obviously guilty murderer who makes a closing speech that plays on the prejudices of the jury – you think he doesn't know what he's doing? Why do you listen to such people? There's always a libertarian principle, exception, inalienable right or point of order to argue. Even I can be defended.'

The Devil pauses and looks around the court.

'I have existed since the dawn of time. Every few hundred years man ruptures his past. Fire is discovered. The wheel is invented. Printing replaces the written word. Steam locomotion industrialises the world. Slavery is abolished. The atom is split. Space is conquered. You need to rupture the law.'

'And why are you telling us this?' the judge asks. 'Why risk ruining your evil handywork?'

'Because you'll never do it,' the Devil replies.

The judge wakes up, regretting that he has no time to analyse a dream in which truth is put into the Devil's mouth. With Cocksacks positioned at every street corner, he smiles at the irony of sharing the same fate as his dream devil.

✧

TOMAS

The biggest problem in the world ever . . .

Tereza's single concern on her final night is for the women of the West. She knows the reputation of Russian men, the soldiers in particular, and giant phalluses with massive distended testicles spell only one thing for womankind.

She dreams of fine white particles falling from the sky like the lightest, most beautiful snow. Instead of coating the earth – buildings, fields, objects, men – the particles only fall on women. Flakes seek out the ones who are indoors. They all find this odd, but don't think much about it and go to bed.

The next morning, women awake to a magic transformation. Everything that was previously impressive, attractive and alluring about men – muscles, money, machismo – has ceased to hold any interest for them. They immediately set out to confirm this strange new feeling.

'I've just closed a big deal,' says a man, 'how about some fun?' The girl looks away, bored. 'Can I take you on my jet?' says another. 'No thank you, I prefer commercial,' the girl replies. An abdomen king struts his stuff on the beach. Three bathing beauties stifle a yawn. 'Let me help you get that part,' a producer offers with a knowing look. 'I'll get it myself,' the one-time 'producee' replies. 'When I was at my house in the South of France . . . ' a banker begins. 'Was that a surreptitious money message?' the girl says cutting him short. 'How vulgar.'

And that's it. In a heartbeat men lose their power over women. A monstrous problem, as big as the planet itself, rears its terrifying head for the first time in human history. How are men going to have sex? Women are now impervious to money talk, boasts, promises, lies; all the clichés of the chase. Catastrophe!

Desperately men scramble to learn manners and interesting topics of conversation, the new weapons of seduction. Finishing schools for men are established in Switzerland. The Queen's butlers give free lessons on how to walk to armies of men on parade grounds. Museums are packed with males, library shelves are cleared. The world internet crashes. All knowledge is vacuumed up. For a time it works. Men manage to hold their own on the new level playing field. Soon, girls have heard all the knowledge and seen all the walks. Just for the hell of it, they turn things up a notch.

A man with great courtesy and not a hint of boastfulness offers a girl a ride on his jet. 'Fine,' she says, 'but you'll have to give it to me.' And do you know what? He does. 'You said before that you were worth €100 million,' says another to a doting admirer. 'I want €10 million. Now.' Immediately he writes a cheque. 'You can take me out for tea,' says a debutante, 'but via Chanel. We'll visit Graffe on the way home.'

Once power has been established, why stop in the middle? Why not go all the way? Although she is asleep, Tereza is conscious of that ancient truism – he who no longer cares has ultimate power. Except that the he is now a she. Within a few years all the money, power and influence in the world has shifted from men to women.

Men now stand naked, gibbering, desperate for sex

before their female masters. It's not difficult to guess what happens next.

First, girls decide to quieten down the world. Like men, it's too noisy. Cars, so precious to men, are the first to go. The substitute form of transport is men in harness with bits in their mouths, pulling rickshaw-like carriages, encouraged by a whip. Thereafter, men are banned from speaking altogether, other than to pay female-approved compliments and answer questions about menial tasks such as: 'Has the house been cleaned since this morning?'

Second, women begin to experiment with having sex without men. Initially they find other methods that are just as pleasurable. Men were never that good, anyway. All that mess, fuss and need for satisfaction. After a while, they start to prefer sex by themselves. This fashion spreads, and soon the female masters no longer copulate with their male slaves. It's a short distance to the final step.

With great thought and care as to selection, sperm is taken from the top academics, artists, scientists and athletes, enough to last an eternity. Women now control births. Naturally, only female embryos are chosen. Within a hundred years men become extinct. Tereza's dream ends with her floating above a planet full of soft colours, marshmallow shapes, high-pitched laughter and girls having cocktails by the sea.

CANNES

A lesson in togetherness . . .

While Reynard and Tereza dream, Tomas meets the Emperor in the grand salon of his fabulous Onion. They sit in candlelight in comfortable armchairs, with magnificent views of the sea and mountains beyond.

Tomas is white with anxiety and shaking uncontrollably. He feels sick. Cocksack paratroopers are falling all over Europe: city squares, street corners, road junctions, stations, ports and airports across the West have been occupied. Soon the Onion will be surrounded. In retrospect, his plan seems mad. Maybe he listened too intently to the Emperor's lessons on risk, failure and mediocrity. In following the first, he is about to give a masterclass in the second two.

'Courage, my friend,' says the Emperor. 'The eve of battle is always the worst. Come, let's speak of something else. Allow me to distract you with a question.'

Tomas stares blankly ahead, immobilised by the coming terror.

'What is the answer to one of life's most difficult problems? How can two people remain together?' the Emperor asks.

Tomas remains silent, unable to think.

'Haven't you noticed a pattern?' the Emperor continues. 'Sexual infatuation followed by immediate coupling; then the magic fades. Once the rabbit is out of the hat, where's the surprise? A creeping mist descends and the couple enter a twilight world where nothing grows. Then it's downhill all the way: rows, recriminations and rudeness.

Lastly, there is heartbreak and pain.'

Tomas is still a frozen blank.

'Come, Tomas,' says the Emperor. 'Is there a trick, or a magic formula? How can this cycle be broken?'

'There should be respect between two people,' Tomas eventually replies.

'And . . . ' says the Emperor.

'You need to be alike and share the same interests.'

'And . . . '

'Integrity's important, as is a sense of humour.'

'There's much in what you say,' replies the Emperor. 'But it is not, alas, the answer. I need one word for everyone to have, a guiding star to happiness.'

The Emperor makes a discreet gesture and a moonbeam touches the edge of Tomas's chair. Tomas immediately fires off a dozen words. 'Love, children, intelligence, consideration, decency, humour, compassion, forgiveness, moderation, truthfulness, tolerance, equality, passion.'

'Those are good words,' the Emperor replies, 'but none of them is right. The answer is . . . ' He pauses to study Tomas's reaction. 'Distance,' he says; 'it's the only way for a relationship to work.'

Tomas shifts in his chair. What cynicism is this? His bombardment of clichés failed to hit the target. But distance? Is it another of the Emperor's contrary opinions?

'Why is it that so many relationships don't work and divorce is at a record high? The answer is simple. At the start, it's all froth and slather, there's no backwards gear. People go crashing in. Weeks, months or years later, there's an accident.'

'What about passion?' asks Tomas.

'Passion's fine if it's part of something else. Otherwise it fades. You know that. But people are swept by its tide, so they blunder from one encounter to the next like a drunk clinging to one lamp-post after another on his way home.'

'Very well,' says Tomas. 'I accept people should be more circumspect at the begining. But why is there a need for distance after that?'

'Take priests,' says Napoleon. 'As you know, intimacy is forbidden to them. They believe that there's a lot to be said for distance.'

'And how do they benefit from it?' Tomas asks.

'By its nature, distance implies a certain reserve, and good manners; not pushing yourself forward. With this comes discipline. Thoughts are measured. Consideration is given. Words are not spoken in anger. And for those to whom intimacy is not forbidden, distance is the enemy of thoughtless couplings, selfish and stupid unions and "Look at me! Look at me on my wedding-day!" '

Tomas understands but asks the Emperor to elaborate.

'What would you say,' Napoleon asks Tomas, 'if one day God waved his hand and an extra room were added to each house in the world with the exclusive purpose of allowing one of the inhabiting couple to escape the other? How often do people long to be alone? How much happier would everyone be if some things were left unsaid? If the rule were politeness, consideration, discretion at all times?'

'But the recipe for a successful relationship is together-ness, to be as one, with all things equally said, done and shared,' says Tomas.

'No, that's a recipe for nausea,' Napoleon replies. 'Of course people should be together, but they also need to be apart. It's the only way.' He gestures for the moonbeam to shine full on Tomas. The new Messiah springs from his seat.

'Emperor, it's my greatest wish that we should meet again,' he says.

'It is mine as well,' Napoleon replies. 'If not in this life, then in my class.'

'A fine notion, isn't it?' Tomas replies. 'You're dead, now go back to school.'

A chance to be more than a great nothing . . .

The funicular railway, built in 1925, is now a ruin of collapsed concrete and rusted cables. The track, which runs a thousand feet to the summit of the hill overlooking Cannes, is covered in undergrowth; the terminus is a graffitied shade of its former glorious self. It's still possible, however, to scramble up the line. The Alien begins his climb before dawn on the night of the Cocksack invasion.

At the same time, eight hundred miles away, the combined fleets of the West are straining against the chains that are attached to Italy's heel. These creak and groan as the ships ride the waves. The sea symphony is extinguished by an ear-splitting crunch as Tomas activates the Taiwanese island-raising technology that he acquired on his adventures, and the foot of Italy detaches from the sea floor and soars into the air.

The Alien reaches the top of the funicular observation

tower just as King Rat begins his countdown to Arma-geddon. The Alien tunes in and synchronises with it and exactly on the count of 'two' he spreads his arms wide and tilts back his head, as if trying to ascend to heaven.

Towards which Italy's foot now floats, connected to the fleet by thousands of chains. The ships sail at full speed, pulling the foot, which is anchored to the earth's core by the giant pin, back to a ninety-degree angle. Tomas urges the fleet on. There's not a minute to lose.

For the Alien, there's not a second to lose. Between the count of 'two' and 'three', he locks his telekinetic power on to the ten million spherical objects that are menacing every square and street corner in Europe. Slowly, they begin to rotate. The phalluses, surprised by this strange interference, ignore the activation command. King Rat orders the Cocksacks to shake off the Alien's hold, then gives another strike order.

If time is racing on the hilltop, it's going at light speed in the Ionian Sea. The foot is now fully retracted, its toe positioned, as if about to give something an almighty kick. The chains strain with the effort of holding it back; anchored by the giant pin, it groans, desperate to be released.

The Cocksacks are also in a frantic struggle. The Alien begins to shake as much as Tomas did when levitating the hotel. The phalluses jump and shuffle, weakening his grip. King Rat sends another activation order. Again they're thrown off balance by the rotation of their equipment and fail to respond. Order after order is given. Ten million Cocksacks leap in unison, shaking the Alien's hold. Just as he feels it slipping, he lets out a piteous cry, which reverberates around the mountains, sending a signal to the new Messiah.

This is it. The pivotal moment. The tipping point. Where risk ends in defeat, or just possibly victory. Where Tomas is in the arena, covered in sweat, blood and filth. Even if he fails, his attempt will be remembered and his place will never be with the fence-sitters, who know neither victory nor defeat. Win, lose or draw, Tomas can savour this moment until death. He'll be remembered as more than just another echo on the wind. A moment like this, he thinks, is one that all men should seek, in the knowledge that life is short and death certain; the chance to be more than a great nothing.

He orders the chains released and turns off the Taiwanese technology. Freed from its manacles, the foot swings down and forward with a terrible velocity. It strikes the ball at the end of Italy's boot, Sicily, with a tremendous force that tears it from the seabed and sends it hurtling into the sky. Instantly, all the volcanoes on the island erupt.

The roar of this conflagration creates a sonic boom, which is heard across Europe and distracts King Rat in his battle of wills against the Alien. Moments later, Rat spies report that, inexplicably, the island of Sicily is airborne and heading north up the Italian peninsula. Considering this strange proposition, King Rat wavers in his command of the Cocksacks. In this split second the Alien seizes the advantage. With one terrible final cry, he pushes his telekinetic powers to the limits of endurance. At last the fulcrum tips. Within moments the Cocksacks' appendages are rotating at the speed of sound. Seconds later they explode. Ten million shattered phalluses now litter the streets of Europe.

Meanwhile, Sicily is tearing north like a comet approaching its crash site. As it passes Rome, bells ring out in salutation and the Pontiff appears on his balcony to cheer and wave. As the island powers over central Europe, the wily Sicilian men distract the women by pointing out the erupting volcanoes. The population is now hanging over the edge for the ride; while the girls look inwards, the boys shout words of love to the Czech beauties below.

On hearing of the paratroopers' annihilation, King Rat calls up the reserve army massed on the Polish border. The loss is devastating but Russia had expected heavy casualties and has survived worse in the past. King Rat swears vengeance; it will come soon, he thinks, as five million fresh phalluses begin to deploy.

The first he hears of the flying landmass is a distant rumbling like an approaching storm. So much the better, he thinks; the army will advance to the sound of thunder. As the sky darkens, King Rat orders the army to break out its waterproof gear. But the gathering gloom signifies more than bad weather. Shortly afterwards the sun fades. Moments later, it is extinguished. What sounded like distant thunder is in fact the roar of something altogether more horrifying – an airborne leviathan ripping the very fabric of the sky.

With incredible speed and dexterity, King Rat scurries from his command post, leaving the massed ranks of phalluses, which begin to jump, bump, fall, wobble, scream and cry. And no wonder. From the ground, all that is

ILLUSTRATION ON
THIS PAGE

9

ILLUSTRATION ON
THIS PAGE

visible is a massive slab of granite and rock spewing fire and smoke. But the sight lasts only seconds. In a heartbeat, five million phalluses are emasculated for ever.

King Rat's revenge . . .

Every few years there's a monster storm, combining hurricane winds, waterfall rain and deafening creaks and groans as things move or fall over. Today, a still louder noise can be heard above the deluge. The Great Bear's roar echoes through the valleys and shakes the snow off the mountain tops.

The Great Bear paces his lair waiting for King Rat, his head jerking in uncontrollable spasms of rage. Just as the echo of his summons subsides, his cave jumps into the air, rocked by a thunder clap. Then a lightning flash knocks out the power. The boulder guarding his lair splinters into a thousand pieces, scattering rock and storm debris around the cave. One moment the Great Bear sees the boulder explode; the next there is a man-sized crate in the entrance of the cave. Seconds later, the crate glides towards him, energised, it seems, by the force of the storm. It comes to rest close to him and its front section falls away.

At first he can see nothing inside but blackness. Then, two red beads glow from its depths. The sides of the crate collapse and King Rat, who is the size of a man, steps out.

King Rat possesses the form of a rodent, but is six feet tall and walks on his back legs. His eyes shine like lighthouse beams. He doesn't speak and has no describable expression. He simply stands in front of the Great Bear, who remains incandescent with rage. He tries to compose his thoughts.

'The time for armies is over,' the Great Bear says, looking in fury at the debris-strewn floor.

King Rat remains impassive, waiting for him to continue.

'We've miscalculated and used a battering ram instead of a stiletto thrust.' The Great Bear pauses. 'Kill him whose words hurt me most,' he spits, unable to say Tomas's name. 'Summon me once . . . '

The Great Bear looks up and King Rat is gone. The power returns, the storm abates. All that remains is the debris all over the floor.

King Rat travels by ghostly galleon, taking the storm with him. The ship moves over land, not water, and it leaves a chill in its wake. Within minutes it reaches Warsaw, freezing King Sigismund off his column. In Prague the Charles Bridge cracks and falls into the Vltava, while Lake Geneva ices over as it passes. The galleon sails over the Alps, the storm gathered at its mast, King Rat hanging from its bow, his red eye-beams illuminating the way.

The galleon comes to rest in Cannes. Seconds later King Rat swings his legs over the gunwale and steps down on to the Croisette. As the storm intensifies, a knife glints in the lightning flash. The rodent draws his obscene tail, all sinew, tendon and bone, into a semi-circle and shaves it with the razor-sharp blade. Standing high on his back feet, he sniffs the rain-drenched air.

Soon afterwards, he is in the entrails of the hotel, the unseen innards of wires, pipes, chutes and shafts that give the monster life. Although very large, he compresses his body into a vent and scuttles along inside sniffing. No one can hear him as he passes through the walls silently.

He finds the room and noiselessly removes the grill of the duct. A flash of lightning through the window reveals a sleeping figure below.

Pierre's moment of truth . . .

Perhaps it was the prospect of death that gave Pierre the jolt he needed. At last, he has pieced it all together and discovered the truth. The story is so combustible that he holds a firestorm in his hands. He has the ability to change the world. Realising the awesome power of truth, he writes to his editor before going to bed on the night of the storm.

Dear Editor [he begins], I'm weak and in a quandary because soon I might succumb to the allure of truth. Truth – that seductive mistress whose diaphanous negligee sends hearts racing, with ebony skin, supple limbs and breasts that protrude just a little.

Don't you think she's overrated? All those scholastic colleges with *veritas* on their heraldic shields. The truth, at all costs truth.

The girl asks, 'How do I look tonight?' Do you reply, 'Like a potato'? It's wartime and the enemy has the advantage. Is this broadcast to the nation? You're sick and will die shortly. Do you really want to know? Other than to finish your best bottles, of course.

Some things are spoken that would best be left

unsaid: the painful questions, perceptive observations, invasive remarks; however truthworthy they may be. If over the stretch of a long marriage a single indiscretion occurs, must it be known? The answer is yes, including the details, the more lurid the better!

Should a zoom lens trap a starlet, the truth of her breasts must be exposed. So should the past of the good politician who committed a schoolboy error twenty years ago. Out with it. As for the loving father who once slept with a man, let the world – and his children – know.

Truth, the golden goddess gleaming in her chariot, served by the wisest judge and lowest paparazzo, appealing to our highest morals and basest instincts. But what of her harsh glare, which incinerates all before it?

This power is given to only one in each generation. A story more powerful than the Cocksack army, a thousand words to change the world.

The instrument of this Armageddon? A small black plastic square on a computer keyboard. I'm going to bed now. Maybe in sleep I'll find the answer. Should I give you the story?

Death of a hero . . .

King Rat has done this many times before. Not for him guns, knives or other crude tools of death. Nor does he use doors, windows, elevators or fire escapes – the assassin's usual means of ingress. All he needs is a duct, a one-inch phial and darkness. The sleeping figure lies with his head on a pillow only a few feet below the vent. King Rat has another special technique. He makes no noise. He doesn't even move. He just waits, for hours if necessary.

The sleeper faces the window, oblivious to the storm. He eventually turns on to his other side. King Rat keeps vigil. The sleeper turns back towards the window, then twists over again. At last he lies on his back, his head cradled in a curved arm. Noiselessly, King Rat reaches for the phial. His victim shifts and smacks his lips. He is about to turn back on to his side but then he adjusts his head on the pillow instead. King Rat senses that the moment is close and unfurls his tail like a waking snake. Just as it arches over his head, it happens. The sleeper opens his mouth.

In a flash the phial is uncorked and a single globule of black liquid is dropped on to the tail. It catches the red of King Rat's eyes, glistening as it travels down its highway of doom. King Rat expertly manoeuvres the deadly passenger to an inch above his victim's lips. With an invisible flick, he delivers the droplet to the back of his throat.

Dawn breaks in a huge sky, washed clean by the storm. The Croisette glistens after the deluge. The waiters barely bother to dry out tables and chairs, knowing that the sun will do it for them. Breakfast smells fill the air. Another perfect Mediterranean day.

The Great Bear arrives in Cannes at first light, carried on King Rat's galleon. This is only the second time that he has left his lair in decades, drawn out to parade his kill. On his journey he ruminates on the turn of the wheel. All the planning, time and cost of creating a great army, when the decapitation of one man was all that mattered. He can even withstand the loss of the Cocksacks. A new supply of their venomous load is already being prepared by his ally the Iranian Hawk. All that remains is for him to make his appearance on Shit TV. The cameras await. After that, the poison will be released. The timing makes no difference. So much better to soften the world with news of the fake Messiah's death and then deliver his annihilating balm.

The Great Bear makes his way up to inspect the body, dispensing with his guard. This is a moment he wishes to savour alone. The bedroom door is ajar and through the crack he glimpses the fake Messiah's corpse lying beneath a sheet on the bed. Next to him a computer screen sits open on a bedside table. He had no idea that he was composing his final words.

The mighty beast pauses in the doorway. The memory of decades of pain and frustration flashes through his mind: the Cold War defeat; the years of hibernation; the start of the fight back; the rise of the fake Messiah; the battle for Shit TV; the destruction of the Cocksack army. And now this. The fake Messiah dead, his broadcast platform ready and a new supply of world-controlling venom arriving soon. Slowly, he pads towards the bed.

He stands over the corpse, his giant paw gripping the hem of the sheet. This is it. His enemy is defeated, his destiny fulfilled; fortune's wheel turns no longer; it is fixed eternally in proclamation of the new Russian power. The rule of the Great Bear.

As he pulls back the sheet, he's shocked by a stabbing pain in his thigh. The surprise of the truth dart is nothing compared to what is beneath the sheet. Pierre lies lifeless before him. As Tomas gestures to his guards to manacle the prisoner and lead him to the cameras, the Great Bear's order – 'Kill him whose words hurt me most' – spoken in anger and haste, comes back to his mind.

The root of all evil . . .

The Shit TV dais is on the beachfront facing the hotel. The deep blue sea forms a contrasting backdrop to the blood red of the Russian flag flying in the breeze behind the speaker's podium. All the cameras and paraphernalia required for a global broadcast are ready. Shit TV, promised a spectacle by King Rat, one that'll change the world, now awaits the star of the show.

The West is confused by the destruction of the Cocksacks. Was it an accident? A joke? A precursor to today's programme? As for Sicily's flattening of the reserve army, what incredible magic was that? Whatever the answer, these unprecedented events have sent the world into a frenzy of intrigue and speculation. All work has stopped. Governments didn't even bother to declare a holiday; the planet has taken one anyway. Now five billion people, the biggest audience of all time, wait to hear the answer.

The Great Bear is conducted to the dais by none other than the new Messiah. 'What's this?' thinks Shit TV's programme director. 'The new Messiah serving the Great Bear? This must be part of the show.' He gives the countdown for the broadcast to begin. Silence descends across the world. The excitement is palpable, like lightning in the air. The biggest broadcast of all time, on the largest network in world history, live from Cannes.

Tomas steps up to the podium. He surveys the bank of whirring cameras for a full thirty seconds. Only when the tension is at breaking point does he lean into the microphone to speak.

'Citizens of the world,' he says. 'We have a first in broadcasting history today. Breaking decades of silence, the Great Bear will speak live on this network. This is an incredible event; and I have the honour of being his interviewer.'

The Great Bear comes into shot.

'Great Bear,' Tomas says. 'The world is holding its breath. There are many unanswered questions.' He pauses, momentarily uncertain that the truth drug will work. 'What was the purpose of your plan?'

The Great Bear grimaces and struggles in his restraints, hidden from the audience by a fur camouflage. But the serum of the truth dart is coursing through his veins, its power too strong to resist.

'To subvert the West,' he replies in a staccato outburst. 'We sent oligarchs with yachts and jetted in prostitutes to incite jealousy and avarice. We bought football teams and extolled the virtues of the "ballers" nihilistic lifestyle. We corrupted bankers – not a difficult task – and other servicers of the rich and turned them into our servants. We silenced our enemies at home and watched the West turn a blind eye in its weakness and moral apathy. We perverted values. Already much has been achieved.'

'We know this,' Tomas replies. 'But what was the

purpose of the Cocksacks?'

'Can't you guess? I'm surprised that you ask. What is the world's most pernicious evil? What corrupts nearly everything and tempts even the good man? For what does a woman forget herself and fall into sin? What is the Devil's currency? What corruption is more sickening than a sewer, more putrid than rotting meat?'

The programme director is uneasy with this line of questioning but continues nevertheless. He orders the cameras to pan in on the Great Bear. His scared face with snarling jaw, mottled fur and black eyes fills every television screen in the world. He pauses, struggling against the truth serum. A look of pain and fury contorts his face. He fights hard, but can't resist, even though the answer's now obvious.

'Money,' he gasps, 'the root of all evil. That was the Cocksack's load. Streams, rivers, oceans of it.'

The global audience exhales a collective gasp. Of course, money. But why this apocalyptic description?

'And the effect of spreading it across the West?' Tomas asks.

'Anarchy, of course,' replies the Great Bear. 'People jumping, crying, screaming and screeching for this manna. And then pushing, punching, clawing and fighting. Finally, killing. The strong overpowering the weak. The man with a handful of notes ambushed by the gang hoovering up the street; the old lady smashed in the face for her single bill.'

'Then what?'

'A deluge of death and destruction; marauding gangs more intoxicated by money than any drink or drug. All perspective lost, normality shattered. Citizens attacked, houses ransacked, cities in chaos. Do you think the armed forces and civic authorities would help? With money raining on them too, they'd be the worst offenders. Global disaster. Hell on earth. Evil annihilating good. Nothing sacred. Nobody safe. A money blast more lethal than radiation, enveloping the planet with its contaminating seed.'

'But . . . What about your Empire?'

'Simple,' the Great Bear replies. 'Empires arise from ashes, don't they? What do I want, a world in perfect working order? And who's easier to control, the good and decent or the evil and venal? Once a man is corrupted, he's a slave to himself. It's not difficult to make him slave to another.'

Tomas reflects on the malign brilliance of the Great Bear's plan. Wars are fought with weapons – but why use them? Why not money? Rain it down and the enemy will annihilate itself. As he imagines clouds of notes billowing in the air, the Great Bear's apocalyptic vision becomes a reality in his mind.

Shit TV's programme director is also agitated. 'Where's this leading?' he thinks. 'Is this really the promised show? Should I pull the broadcast?'

Tomas is quick with his next question. 'What about the amount of money needed?' he asks. 'How could the supply possibly endure?'

'The pipeline to our friend and neighbour the Iranian Hawk,' the Great Bear replies. 'He gave us oil in return for technology and our support for his madness in the world. Also . . . ' The Great Bear battles against the serum. Today he's defeated, but if he can just conceal this detail, maybe one day, decades hence, the wheel will turn and he'll have his revenge.

Tomas wonders how the Iranian pipeline alone could produce the billions needed for the Great Bear's plan. But he dismisses the thought and is about to ask another question when he remembers Pierre's article about the pipeline extension – a secret Pierre never managed to expose.

'Where does the pipeline end?' Tomas asks.

The Great Bear inhales deeply. He clenches his teeth and pulls a hideous grimace, forcing his mouth to lock. He begins to shake his head from side to side, looking demented. The programme director almost cuts the feed.

'Where does the pipeline end?' Tomas repeats.

'In Iraq, of course,' the Great Bear spits out at lightning speed. 'Just over the border from Iran, in the biggest oilfields in the world. Why do you think we've fomented trouble in the region for decades, feeding the flames of Western policy and encouraging Iran to ever greater extremes? Obviously, it was to distract attention from our activities.'

'How is this possible?' Tomas asks stupefied.

'Very easily,' the Great Bear replies, 'it's a lot less difficult than flying to the moon. A pipeline is just a subterranean tunnel dug with machines. It is also impossible to detect: satellites can't see underground. Oil is abundant in the area, with deep reserves stretching across borders. We've acquired billions of barrels while you've been busy chasing shadows. And what's the worst that can happen? You find out and ask for it back.'

Tomas is amazed. Of all man's thefts of land, people, power and riches in history, this is the most simple and devious. Technologically easy and impossible to detect, taking advantage of a unique combination of circumstances. That the scheme went so far and lasted so long was testimony to the madness of the world.

The idea of dementia triggers a final question in Tomas's mind. 'What was Shit TV's role?' he asks.

Instantly the programme director moves to cut the satellite signal, but the Alien locks the network's satellites. No interference is possible. Five billion people hear his answer.

'What do morons eating live bugs in the jungle create? Other morons. And fools in a house airing their infantile opinions? More fools. Masochists being abused by foul-mouthed chefs and smooth-tongued judges? Yet more masochists. Shit TV was the invisible cancer, more lethal than venom, more corrosive than acid. It turned minds into mush. Its daily dose made the world sicker and weaker. A world of morons, fools and masochists, but for you, powerless in my hands.'

In commemoration of Shit TV's final broadcast, the Alien rotates its satellites until they become a silver soup that sparkles in space.

A dead man's story . . .

As the Great Bear makes his first and final appearance on Shit TV, the Prefect of Police arrives at the murder scene. He undertakes a perfunctory examination of the room, while awaiting the arrival of the forensic experts, and notices the journalist's computer on the bedside table. He presses a key. Pierre's letter to his editor about 'truth' is displayed, the story to which it refers attached. He moves the cursor to read the story. Then a glint catches his eye. Through a half-opened door, he notices a wonderland of mirrors: the floor-to-ceiling arrangement found in expensive bathrooms. A story to change the world or an opportunity to adjust his cap in this paradise of reflective surfaces? The choice is easy. He is just completing his millinery toilette when Judge Reynard arrives. For some time he's been concerned about Pierre's investigations; on hearing of his murder, he wanted to be the first to look around.

The judge takes in the scene with the expert eye of an evidence-gatherer. He's seen it all before. Within minutes, he has read Pierre's letter.

'Monsieur le Préfet,' says Judge Reynard, 'I shall require this computer for examination.'

'Bien sûr, Monsieur le Juge,' replies the prefect, raising his cap.

Judge Reynard sits in a comfortable chair in the salon of Tomas's apartment. Pierre's computer is on his lap. He presses the 'on' button and it whirs into life. What is this story that will change the world? Did he discover the secret of the pipeline before his death? Is this his valedictory piece? In his heart, the judge knows it isn't. He muses for a moment on the thread that separates success from failure, victory from defeat. The Great Bear had this story within his grasp. His simple mistake was to go to Pierre's room unguarded, wishing, no doubt, to savour his moment of triumph alone. If it hadn't been for this small hubristic act, he would now be reading the story to the world live on Shit TV, the new Messiah his prisoner in chains.

Reynard finds Pierre's letter and the story attachment beneath. Would Pierre have sent the article in the morning? People often feel different in the cold light of day. Pierre's urge to reveal the 'truth', so enhancing to his reputation and riches, might have faltered on reflection. The judge presses a key and Pierre's final piece appears on screen. Reynard sits back in his armchair and starts to read:

> The story begins with a brilliant young man, Emile Reynard, training to become a doctor. He quickly masters the rudiments of medicine, but feels called to a wider role in life. On becoming a lawyer, he rises through the judicial ranks to become the country's foremost judge, noted for dispensing wise and robust justice. He retires with his mental faculties intact but also, alas, with a terminal disease. But he's brought back by the Supreme Justices to try Tomas's case. Only the most senior judiciary will do. This much we know.
>
> The story takes a twist during Tomas's trial. On reading the transcript it is clear that Reynard, far from being hostile to Tomas, is sympathetic to him. From this, it's reasonable to suspect that the judge also believes that the means justifies the end. Perhaps, after a lifetime's exposure to evil, Reynard takes the

same view on society as Tomas. Although appalled by Tomas's morality lessons, he has little sympathy for their recipients.

Reynard considers Tomas's death sentence by popular demand to be even more abhorrent than his crimes and against every legal principle. Not being a fence-sitter, he decides to take matters into his own hands. The judge personally interviews and selects the soldiers for Tomas's execution squad and oversees all details of his execution. We also know that the others chosen to attend – the vulture and the buzzard – were nonentities, who have since disappeared. And that the judge, meticulous in every detail, surprisingly failed to make arrangements for the internment of Tomas's body following his death.

The judge is immediately to hand after Tomas's resurrection and assigns a battalion to guard him, an unusual decision. He connives in the general frenzy surrounding Tomas's deitific status. He continues to support Tomas as he inverts an historic monument and builds a new one. All this based on the simple premise of Tomas's resurrection. Except that Tomas didn't rise from the dead. He awoke from sleep.

Tomas speaks of a swirling sensation in his veins after he was shot, followed by sleep: the description of an anaesthetic taking effect. The soldiers were not Tomas's executioners but his anaesthetists. More precisely, one was. Instead of five guns loaded with live ammunition and one empty, it's likely that all were blank except one that contained an anaesthetic dart. How was this achieved? Like all brilliant plans, with great simplicity. The squad was hypnotised by the judge, who is an accomplished psychohypnotist from his medical days. Reynard simply found the six most vulnerable to his technique: 'Close your eyes, my son, search your heart.'

This theory was confirmed by the insusceptibility of the smoker in the squad to hypnosis. I went for treatment to help me quit and subsequently gave the hypnotist's name to the smoking soldier. Later, I received a message that the soldier's head was 'blocked'. Someone had been there first.

The rest, as they say, is history. Tomas has pursued an agenda of social change, no doubt influenced by the judge. Tomasmania is an unexpected bonus for Reynard's plan. Even without this, he has had a global platform from which to raise the debate, particularly with regard to justice, where the judge's lifelong experience of the silver-tongued techniques of lawyers has radicalised his views. Doubtlessly, he does not expect to succeed in changing the system. But maybe lighting a fire is enough. One day the law might just 'rupture'.

It's remarkable but true that sometimes the oldest and least suspect people can surprise. The genius professor quietly working on a world-changing formula in his laboratory; the brilliant academic silently making a remarkable discovery. With age and experience come stealth and cunning – far more potent than young men shouting or burning flags in the street. Judge

TOMAS

Reynard is the perfect, perhaps the ultimate, exemplar. What is the worst that could happen? Prison? Unlikely: the State would suppress the plot in order to preserve the honour and financial position of the *Patrie*. In any event, Reynard is old and knows he will die shortly. And the best result? It's already happened. A global reaction against Russian roubles, bankers' bonuses and football filth.

The only remaining question is whether Tomas was hypnotised as well? The answer is almost certainly yes. After his 'execution' we know Reynard spent time privately with him. It's also reasonable to speculate that there were other occasions on which the judge could practise his art. But it doesn't actually matter whether Tomas was hypnotised or not. The power of belief is greater than any hypnotic spell. And Tomas's conviction that he was the second Messiah made him ready putty in the hands of the puppet master.

So where does this end? That will be for you, my readers, to say. You may wish to continue to believe. Tomas's influence has spread far and wide. This is the nature of a new religion. It arises, catches fire, then there's a counter reaction. My purpose is to reveal the truth. But this may be apostasy to Tomas's supporters. One man's truth is another man's lie; one man's god, another man's devil. What does it matter what we believe, or even if our beliefs are absurd? The Romans had their gods; others worship the fairies in the woods. I have shone the light. You must now decide.

CANNES

Judge Reynard closes his eyes. A kindly, tired old man hunched in a chair. Perhaps he's reflecting on life. Or maybe he has just fallen asleep. His finger hovers over another small black plastic square with 'delete' written on it. A moment later, he goes to join his friends on the balcony.

Sunset over the sea . . .

Tomas and Tereza are sitting on a sofa watching the sunset. Reynard settles on a lounger beside them while the Alien twirls around the balcony amusing himself. Tereza is drinking champagne, the bottle propped in a bucket on the floor nearby. Tomas has an ice-cold beer. Reynard takes a campari and soda, an old man's drink. In front of them is a basket of crudités – the sort you can only get in the Mediterranean – and a dish of oil mixed with mustard, salt and pepper.

Tomas has always loved the light in the South of France. All skies are different, but the atmosphere along this coast is somehow unique. Neither too harsh, like the northern light, nor oppressive like the sun-laden skies further south, it's a perfect blend of colour and heat; and the light show's climactic glory is, of course, the sunset.

There's something satisfying about a seaside town winding down for the day. Loungers and all the beach paraphernalia are being cleaned and stacked away. Bars opening; sunbathers smelling of coconut oil returning to their hotels; waiters preparing for the evening service. This is the moment of calm between the day's end and the night's activities.

TOMAS

The sunset is a symphony of clouds and colours. Yellow turns to orange, then deep red, the sky shot through with a kaleidoscope of colours as the sun moves lower on the horizon. With every breeze, the painted clouds change shape and size like dancers at a phantasmic ball.

The invisible voice joins the party with his friend the invisible eye, who has a special perspective on the sunset. 'What can you see?' says the invisible voice. The invisible eye looks through the colours and clouds to the very innards of the sky. Sure enough he sees billions of echoes on the wind, but every so often a great man in history – Julius Caesar, the Emperor Charlemagne, Napoleon Bonaparte . . . Dancing among them, like a kite on the breeze, he glimpses a familiar, still living face.

Tomas looks across the terracotta roofs of the city to the back of the beachside hotels, the sea and the mountains beyond. The sea is a deepening blue against the mountains, which look like cardboard cut-outs against the sky as the light fades. The sun makes its final descent. For a moment, a giant red ball perches ethereally on the mountain top. Then it quickly slips below. A furnace ignites on the far mountainside, shooting red flames into the clouds, which continue their spectral dance.

Tomas takes in the scene in silence, holding Tereza's hand on the sofa. He hopes that, at his end, should it come quickly, he'll be given just a few minutes to remember the indescribable beauty of this moment.